P9-DVI-085

First Christians

Books by Paul L. Maier

A MAN SPOKE, A WORLD LISTENED

PONTIUS PILATE

FIRST CHRISTMAS

FIRST EASTER

FIRST CHRISTIANS

First Christians

PENTECOST
AND THE SPREAD OF CHRISTIANITY

Paul L. Maier

1817

HARPER & ROW, PUBLISHERS

NEW YORK, HAGERSTOWN, SAN FRANCISCO, LONDON

HIEBERT LIBRARY
Pacific College WITHDRAWN
Fresno, Calif. 93702

14539

For
MABEL E. BRECKENKAMP
and
NORMA H. BELLMANN
sisters I never had

ACKNOWLEDGMENTS

Grateful acknowledgment is made to the following for permission to reprint selections included in this book:

HARVARD UNIVERSITY PRESS for quote from H. Feldman's translation of Josephus, *Antiquities* xix, 8, 2 in the *Loeb Classical Library*.

CHRISTIAN HERALD MAGAZINE for discussion which first appeared in Paul L. Maier, "Tongues Have Been Here Before," *Christian Herald*, 98 (October, 1975), 16-22.

THE LUTHERAN WITNESS for permission to use material which first appeared in Paul L. Maier, "Acts 17: God Comes to Mars' Hill," *The Lutheran Witness*, 93 (June 16, 1974), 8-9.

Biblical quotations in this book, where identified, are from the *Revised Standard Version*, which is copyright 1946 and 1952 by the Division of Christian Education of the National Council of the Churches of Christ in the United States of America. Several Biblical citations initialed NEB are from the *New English Bible*, and TEV from *Today's English Version*.

Bible references in the text that have only chapter and verse indicated are from the *Acts of the Apostles*. So as not to clutter the text, such references usually identify only the verse where the scene or episode *begins* in the New Testament, and the "ff." is omitted.

Photographs are by the author, except for the first, which is published by permission of NASA.

FIRST CHRISTIANS: *Pentecost and the Spread of Christianity.* Copyright © 1976 by Paul L. Maier. All rights reserved. Printed in the United States of America. No part of this book may be used or reproduced in any manner whatsoever without written permission except in the case of brief quotations embodied in critical articles and reviews. For information address Harper & Row, Publishers, Inc., 10 East 53rd Street, New York, N.Y. 10022. Published simultaneously in Canada by Fitzhenry & Whiteside Limited, Toronto.

FIRST EDITION

Library of Congress Cataloging in Publication Data

Maier, Paul L
    First Christians.
    Includes bibliographical references.
    1. Church history—Primitive and early church, ca. 30–600. I. Title.
BR165.M26 1976   270.1   75-36751
ISBN 0-06-065399-X

Contents

Illustrations

COLOR PLATES

Following page   32

Preface

This book completes my trilogy on the major festivals of the Christian church in their original setting. As with *First Christmas* and *First Easter,* these pages supplement the New Testament account with findings from ancient history and archaeology, as well as evidence from the languages, law, economics, geography, and even climatology of Mediterranean antiquity. I am pleased that such an approach has been well received by both critics and the general public in the first two volumes of this series.

Much as *First Easter* was inseparably linked to events which happened *before* that momentous Sunday, the first Christian Pentecost finds its proper perspective in what occurred *after* that festival in a rapid spread of the faith. I regret that space restrictions prevent more than cursory glances into the theology of Peter and Paul, to which, of course, many separate commentaries have been devoted.

The *Acts of the Apostles* provides much of the framework in the text, and most references without further identification, (1:6) for example, refer to Acts. Other sources are documented in the Notes at the end of the book.

Western Michigan University   P.L.M.

9

1

The Commission

"But you shall receive power when the Holy Spirit has come upon you; and you shall be my witnesses in Jerusalem and in all Judea and Samaria and to the end of the earth."

ACTS 1:8

One would have thought that the resurrection of Jesus of Nazareth was the ultimate proof necessary to launch Christianity upon the world. But it was not.

Had mortal authors conjured up this story, they could hardly have resisted a scenario in which the risen Christ paid a victorious visit to Pilate, Caiaphas, the Sanhedrin, and the Jerusalem mob, finally compelling them to believe what they formerly had not. The fright, the awe, the hysterical pleading for forgiveness would have made high drama, and waves of now-universal adulation would have splashed as far away as Rome and converted the Empire. But Jesus made no such appearances to his enemies after the first Easter, which was entirely in accord with divine policy: God never rewards disbelief; he always rewards faith.

Instead, then, the great Good News would have to be communicated by people who had witnessed the Easter phenomenon, not by endless theophanies of the risen Christ to prove the case. But could the witnesses—unaided—handle such an assignment? One doubts. The record of the disciples surely leaves nothing to boast about. Their somewhat naïve question even *after* the Resurrection—"Lord, will you at this time re-

11

store the [political] kingdom to Israel?" (1:6)—shows precious little theological progress on their part.

Enter the Holy Spirit. Jesus repeatedly foresaw the problem of a message too powerful for the messengers, and so he told the disciples at the Last Supper: "I will not leave you desolate. . . . the Counselor, the Holy Spirit, whom the Father will send in my name, he will teach you all things, and bring to your remembrance all that I have said to you" (Jn. 14:18). That person and function of God which would convict and convert people, inspire and propel them, would shortly transform the apostles from timid, passive, dull, and generally ineffective followers of Jesus into courageously powerful heralds in his behalf.

The Spirit's arrival would be anchored to a specific time and place in the first instance. After Jesus left them, the disciples were not to leave Jerusalem but rather wait there for the Spirit. The Day of Pentecost would mark his dramatic arrival, even if the apostles could not know that.

THE DEPARTURE

Forty final days the risen Jesus spent with his followers—a number sacred since the Flood. Then he prepared to take leave of them.

Only Luke reports the Ascension in any detail. Jesus led the Eleven over the Mount of Olives toward Bethany, the village where he had lived during the week before his crucifixion. His last message to them was both blessing and assignment, a solemn commission to do what must have seemed overblown and impossible at the time: to spread his story across the entire world! The other Gospels echo this categorical goal:

> ". . . make disciples of all nations" (Matthew)
> "Go into all the world and preach the gospel
>   to the whole creation." (Mark)

"... preached in his name to all nations, beginning from Jerusalem" (Luke)

Such phrases forever set the New Testament apart from
other books. Certainly, they are unparalleled in the ancient
world. No dying philosopher ever uttered so all-embracing a
charge to his followers, nor did any world conqueror. The best
that Augustus of Rome could manage for his last words was a
witty borrowing from Greek theater: "Have I played my part
in life's farce well enough? Then clap your hands and take me
off the stage." Other "famous last words" are not much more
profound than this.

Jesus, however, was not dying. He was rather establishing an
almost limitless objective for Christianity, and the only thing
more amazing than the words themselves is the fact that they
have been *fulfilled*. With the current expansion of the Christian faith across the world, the Great Commission has proved
to be great prophecy as well.

When the inexorable moment arrived, Jesus raised his hands
in benediction, departed majestically from all terrestrial limita-
tions, and disappeared from view. A bright cloud interposed
between Jesus and his followers—some have seen it as the same
"pillar of cloud" that protected Israel from the Egyptians in
the Exodus account—but when it dissolved, Jesus was gone.

The Ascension should never be interpreted in quantifying
terms. Incredibly, some have speculated on Jesus' rate of as-
cent, the spectacular sight of a Christ figure getting ever
smaller in the heavens to human view, and whether or not it
would have caused any commotion in nearby Jerusalem! This
is not Luke's purpose, which was merely to tell of Jesus' transit
to another dimension, in more modern terms. Even Jesus'
direction "upward" serves only to emphasize his physical sepa-
ration from the earth, not a specific vector away from it.

Predictably, the disciples' only reaction to the stupefying
visual phenomenon was simply to stand there, gazing after it.
Was it awe? The realization that Jesus actually *was* parting

from them? Bewilderment at their leaderless situation? The voices of two bystanders "in white robes" restored their senses: "Men of Galilee, why do you stand looking into heaven? This Jesus, who was taken up from you into heaven, will come in the same way as you saw him go into heaven" (1:11).

Precisely *where* all this took place is not definite. Luke writes only that it was on the Mount of Olives, "a sabbath day's journey away" from Jerusalem, which would be about half a mile. Any point along or near the present ridge of the Mount of Olives would qualify, and only the gullible will believe that the two footprints in stone shown pilgrims today at the hilltop mark "the last steps of Jesus on earth."

A UNIQUE SOURCE

With the Ascension, Luke begins his great story of the spread of Christianity, the account of how a faith born in the hills of Judea would penetrate the imperial capital of Rome 1,500 miles away in a stunningly brief period of time. By many standards, our chief source for this record is unique among Biblical authors. Luke is the only writer of Scripture to produce both a Gospel and that earliest church history known as the *Acts of the Apostles.* But more: Luke is the *only* Gentile author in that library of sixty-four other Semitic books called the Bible. He had a personal interest, then, in telling how the faith overcame its Jewish restrictiveness to embrace also the Gentile world.

Luke, an affectionate form of the Latin Lucius or Lucanus, was a close companion of Paul and an eyewitness to many of the events he described. By training a physician, Luke seems to have sublimated his profession to what he deemed a more pressing priority, and turned to the pen instead. The church is poorer for not having more solid information on Luke. Even his native country is uncertain, although early tradition favors either Antioch in Syria or Philippi in Macedonia as his home town. The autobiographical details Luke could so easily have provided he did not supply, perhaps intentionally, since he wanted nothing personal to detract from his Gospel or his history.

Some critical scholars have debated whether the author of Luke-Acts actually *was* Luke, and have substituted terms such as "the author of the Third Gospel," "the diarist," and the like. Yet no other name for the writer of these works has ever been successfully offered, and the evidence is strong that Luke was the author indeed. Other sources for the earliest spread of Christianity include the letters of Paul and the other apostles, surviving works of first-century Jewish, Greek, and Roman historians, and, to be sure, archaeology. Such evidence blends well into Luke's record, as we shall see.

"You shall be my witnesses in Jerusalem and in all Judea and Samaria and to the end of the earth," Jesus had predicted in his last charge on the Mount of Olives. These words serve as the simple, solemn outline for the entire Book of Acts, and Luke begins his record with the Spirit's dramatic arrival in Jerusalem ten days after the Ascension.

2

The Day of Pentecost

So those who received his word were baptized, and there were added that day about three thousand souls.

ACTS 2:41

Before Pentecost there were only 120 Christians in Jerusalem, and their gathering place was a large "upper room," otherwise unidentified, but probably the same chamber where Jesus had instituted the Last Supper. An early tradition places the Upper Room in southwestern Jerusalem outside the present Zion Gate, but the structure shown tourists today is very disappointing: a gloomy chamber with Gothic vaulting which could not possibly have witnessed the first Christian Pentecost, because the Gothic arch was not developed until the twelfth century A.D. The site, however, may be more authentic, since the structure has been heavily rebuilt across the centuries.

Who were the 120 first Christians? The disciples, now twelve again with Matthias replacing Judas, the suicide; the Galilean followers of Jesus, including the Seventy (Lk. 10:1); his mother Mary and his half-brothers (or relatives) who had now converted to the faith; Mary, Martha, Lazarus, and the Bethany contingent; plus miscellaneous Judean followers, such as the Emmaus disciples, John Mark, and his mother. Small in number, they nevertheless formed the nucleus of the most powerful movement ever to develop in history. Their mood was one of prayerful waiting for the Spirit, for they could not know the time and place of his arrival.

The eastern face of the Temple in Jerusalem, as reconstructed in a model designed by Prof. M. Avi-Yonah. To the upper left is the Palace of Herod, where Pilate condemned Jesus, and at the extreme right is one of the towers of the Antonia fortress, where Peter and Paul were imprisoned.

Before the destruction of their Temple in 70 A.D. the Jews had three great "pilgrim festivals" which drew the pious from all parts of Palestine, and, indeed, the Mediterranean world, to Jerusalem. They were the Passover, the Festival of Weeks, and the Feast of Booths. The Weeks festival was also called the Feast of Harvest or the Day of Pentecost (Greek for "the fiftieth"), since it fell exactly fifty days after the wave offering of the sheaf of barley during Passover (Lev. 23:9). Very much akin to the American Thanksgiving Day, Pentecost was an agricultural festival celebrated seven weeks after the harvest season began—hence Festival of "Weeks"—when the first fruits of the *wheat* harvest were presented to God as the source of fertility, in accord with Scriptural directives (Lev. 23:15).

It was most likely the morning of May 25 in the year 33 A.D. that Jerusalem woke to what would be a very special Pentecost. Throngs were soon converging on the Temple mount to watch the chief priests prepare not only their regular sacrifices, but also the special cereal offering of Pentecost. Probably it was the high priest himself, Joseph Caiaphas, who formally picked up two loaves of bread, baked with flour milled from the new wheat crop, and solemnly waved them back and forth in front of the altar as an offering to God in behalf of his people. He was careful not to touch the altar with the loaves, because they had been baked with leaven and would therefore be eaten afterward by the priests. Two lambs without blemish were also presented as a wave offering and sacrificed to the Lord who had made the harvest possible.

All Jewish males attending were then invited to do an altar dance in the courts of the Temple, during which they sang the Hallel, joyous praises from Psalms 113 to 118. Later in the day they might make individual presentations of the first fruits from their own harvests to priests on duty in the Temple, and finally join in the communal meals to which the poor and the strangers in the city were also welcome.

Elsewhere that morning, diagonally across Jerusalem to the southwest, many in the Christian nucleus had gathered for prayer in the Upper Room. Suddenly, about 9 A.M., the place sounded like the foredeck of a ship in a storm. A noise "like the rush of a mighty wind" swept into the chamber, filling the entire house with its whistling roar. Even more astonishing was the visual phenomenon that followed the wind: "tongues, as of fire" appeared to rest on each of the believers at the only flammable part of their bodies—the hair—and yet harmlessly.

Whether the flames were actual or only apparent is not clear, but a word study on "fire" in the Old Testament shows that flames regularly denoted theophany, an appearance of God, ranging from Moses' burning bush and the protective pillar of fire in the Exodus account to the giving of the Law at Mt. Sinai. Fire signified the purifying presence of God.

The wind and the tongues of flame were the externals marking a profound personal revolution in each of the Christians in the Upper Room, for now at last, the Holy Spirit had made his dramatic entry into their lives. Yet how could they be certain of so subjective an experience? And even if they could be certain about it, how could others believe it?

FOREIGN TONGUES

By recourse to the supernatural. Jesus had regularly demonstrated the authority of his message by performing not tricks but useful miracles, and now the Spirit would do the same. Unlettered Galilean fisherfolk and commoners began speaking fluently in foreign languages they had never learned, but which would be very important for their future mission work. They were being understood by Jewish and proselyte celebrants of Pentecost from fourteen different countries ranging from Mesopotamia to Rome, most of whom had probably prolonged their pilgrimage from Passover to include the second great Jewish festival fifty days later. Luke's list of nationalities covers virtually all countries in the eastern Mediterranean except for Galilee, Syria, Cilicia, and Greece, but a total listing would have seemed contrived.

Critics have tried to diminish the number of languages spoken at the first Christian Pentecost to essentially two—Aramaic and Greek, which the disciples and their hearers would already have known—but this does violence to Luke's text, which plainly reports the foreigners' reaction: "We hear them telling in our own tongues the mighty works of God" (2:11).

Such an incredible phenomenon could only attract a growing throng of the curious in always-crowded Jerusalem. Many were able to hear their own national languages plainly above what must have been a din of foreign tongues, while others, particularly at the periphery, might well have heard only a confusing melange of sounds. They would have been the first to drench the event with soggy ridicule. "These men are filled with new wine!" they mocked.

This beverage, in the original Greek, is *gleukos,* meaning "sweet new wine," from which our word "glucose" is derived. New wine in Palestine did not convey a faster intoxication— older wine, in fact, was stronger—but it was a cheap beverage and common fare for drunks. More expensive vintages were often diluted with water, especially among the Greeks and Romans, and so the taunt might have meant, in essence: "These babblers here have guzzled the *cheap* stuff, taken *straight!"*

During Jesus' ministry Simon Peter always seemed to have volunteered the first word whenever the Master stopped teaching or preaching. That it was often a wrong word did not seem to have fazed the strong, lovable, impetuous fisherman. After a gentle scolding from Jesus, Peter would be back again, posing the first question, offering the first opinion—or drawing the first sword.

So it was absolutely in character for Peter to speak first when the disciples were taunted for drunkenness. Probably using Aramaic—the everyday language of Palestine—Peter stood up to address the multitude. He began by meeting the charge of too much alcohol head on: "These men are *not* drunk, as you suppose, since it is only the third hour of the day!" Even drunks would hardly start indulging as early as nine o'clock in the morning. More likely they would be sleeping off the effects of the night before.

No longer groping between faith and misunderstanding now that the Spirit was inspiring him, Peter went on to deliver a masterpiece of an address. In less than a quarter of an hour he managed to root the Pentecost experience and the mission of Christ in Old Testament prophecy—the only way to convince pious Jews of anything. Without resorting to any diplomatic niceties, Peter then stung his hearers for their involvement in the events of Good Friday: "This Jesus . . . you crucified and killed by the hands of lawless men" (2:23). But in closing he announced the way of salvation with the same sublime simplicity that had always characterized it:

Repent, and be baptized every one of you in the name of Jesus Christ
for the forgiveness of your sins; and you shall receive the gift of the
Holy Spirit. For the promise is to you and to your children and to
all that are far off, every one whom the Lord our God calls to him
(2:38).

Anyone reading Peter's sermon in the second chapter of
Acts is overcome with the dramatic personality transformation
it reflects. To be sure, Peter had shown moments of boldness
before—the Rock, as Jesus named him, did have some solid
credits, though generally it was fissured with flaws. Waves on
the Sea of Galilee, the taunts of a servant girl at the palace of
Caiaphas, or Jesus' trial on Good Friday could turn the Rock
into jelly, as he cursed and swore away his relationship to Jesus
and even abandoned him. How could he now surmount so
triumphantly the same challenges that had earlier overcome
him?

The Spirit. In Luke's record the miracle of Pentecost was
not primarily rushing sounds, tongues of flame, or instant lin-
guistic genius, but the arrival of God the Holy Spirit who could
inspire and transform a man in such a way. And even this was
only half the miracle.

THE RESPONSE

constituted the other half. The story of Pentecost closes with
an all-but-incredible statistic: "So those who received his word
were baptized, and there were added that day about three
thousand souls" (2:41). And these were not fly-by-night converts toying with Christianity for a time, but totally committed
Christians, as the context makes clear—a reaction unparalleled
for the fledgling faith. Not even Jesus' preaching drew such a
response, at least not in Jerusalem, or there would have been
more believers than the lonesome 120 Christians before Pentecost.

And this was only the beginning. One day soon afterward,
when Peter and John went up to the Temple for midafternoon

prayer, they healed a beggar at the Beautiful Gate who had been crippled from his birth forty years before. The helpless victim had been a familiar fixture at the Temple—one sees dozens of his cousins-in-misery throughout the Near East today —and so his healing caused an instant sensation and an immediate crowd.

Peter seized the opportunity to deliver an even more impressive version of the Christian message, with this extraordinary result: "Many of those who heard the word believed; and the number of the men came to about five thousand" (4:4), suggesting an adult Christian membership of perhaps twice this number, including, astonishingly, "a great many of the priests" who were "obedient to the faith" in the weeks to come (6:7).

Is such a growth curve for earliest Christianity (120 → 3,000 → 5,000 plus) credible? Critics have challenged the figures in Acts, pointing out how often ancient authors tended to exaggerate numbers. Luke's statistics should be divided by a factor of perhaps ten, some argue, since a Jerusalem with five or ten thousand Christians would be far too high a Christian-Jewish ratio.

This may be true for the normal population of the Holy City, but many of the converts at Pentecost and the days afterward seem to have been pilgrims, visitors, or temporary sojourners who at least tripled the normal Jerusalem population of some 50,000 during the high festivals. The first-century Jewish historian Josephus would have us believe that as many as 3,000,000 were in Jerusalem at such times, but most scholars reduce his claim to several hundred thousands. Against this statistic, however, Luke's figures are not that extreme.

But were there actually that many converts? What is simpler than hanging a zero or two onto a statistic? Wouldn't a little padding be appropriate for Luke's success story? Not really. There is a fascinating datum of evidence from a purely pagan source attesting to the rapid spread and growth of the earliest church. One of the most respected Roman source historians,

Cornelius Tacitus, wrote the following statement about Nero's first great persecution of the Christians at Rome in 64 A.D.:

To suppress the rumor [that he had set fire to Rome], Nero fabricated as culprits, and punished with the most refined cruelties a notoriously depraved class of people whom the crowd called "Christians." The originator of the name, Christus, had been executed in the reign of Tiberius by the governor of Judea, Pontius Pilatus. . . . First, the self acknowledged members of the sect were arrested. Then, on their information, a vast multitude was condemned. . . .

The startling phrase, of course, is the "vast multitude" of Roman Christians persecuted. For Tacitus the Latin *multitudo ingens*, while indefinite, elsewhere suggests numbers in the high hundreds at the very least, and because he detested the Christians and would thus have no interest in stretching his figures on them, ancient historians generally take Tacitus at face value. His is positive evidence from a hostile source and is therefore unusually strong and convincing.

This evidence, in turn, has an obviously important bearing on conversion claims at the first Pentecost. How could there be a "vast multitude" of Christians available for persecution *only thirty-one years later* in a Rome 1,500 miles away unless the movement had the kind of powerful ignition described in Acts? Any historian would have to admit that a profound religious explosion must have occurred in Jerusalem some years earlier, since its repercussions shook distant Rome with extraordinary speed. For a philosophy or teaching to spread this far, this fast in the ancient world is absolutely unparalleled, and scholars have not devoted enough attention to this fact. Clearly, the spiritual waves breaking on the shores of Italy had been building from the "rushing, mighty wind" of the first Pentecost.

Perhaps even more important than the *numbers* of converts after Peter's preaching were the *kinds* of converts. As noted, the new believers seem to have come largely from the ranks of the pilgrims, visitors, or temporary sorts sojourning in Jerusalem at Pentecost, which had obvious implications for the quick seeding of Christianity across the whole Mediterranean basin. For when these Passover-Pentecost pilgrims returned to their homelands, they would *carry their new faith with them.*

The city of Rome itself is a prime example of such a self-seeding Christianity. When some years later Paul addressed his famous letter to the Christians there, he paid them a high compliment: "I thank my God . . . for all of you, because your faith is proclaimed in all the world" (Rom. 1:8). But who planted this vigorous faith? Neither he, nor Peter, nor any of the apostles had brought Christianity to Italy, even though both Peter and Paul would visit there in the future. Most church historians therefore suggest Pentecost pilgrims—"visitors from Rome, both Jews and proselytes" (2:10)—as the originators of the church at Rome. That church, in turn, would found many other mission stations in the West in a swelling spiritual chain reaction set off, unquestionably, from the original detonation at Pentecost.

Peter, accordingly, could not have addressed a more important audience than the crucial pilgrim Jews of the dispersion, many of whom became human fuses sparking Christianity elsewhere in the ancient world. But if the effect was there—conversion—so was the cause: the arrival of a Spirit who would inspire both speakers and hearers to the faith, governing both ends of the communication process. This alone could explain the extraordinary success of Peter's preaching. This was the true miracle and the ultimate significance of the first great Christian Pentecost.

3

The Opposition

But the high priest rose up and all who were with him, that is, the party of the Sadducees, and filled with jealousy, they arrested the apostles and put them in the common prison.

ACTS 5:17–18

A swift crackdown from the priestly authorities was inevitable. The apostles were not starting their movement in far-off Galilee, but, almost brazenly, they were proclaiming the faith from the very steps of the Temple in Jerusalem. Peter, John, and the others seem to have converted Solomon's Portico on the eastern edge of the Temple enclave into something of a primitive Christian church. Here they preached and healed the sick in a virtual continuation of Jesus' ministry, all under the very noses of the priestly establishment.

Obviously, their activities could not remain unnoticed, and the Temple authorities would hardly have prosecuted Jesus to the cross only to allow his movement to use their facilities as a breeding ground. What particularly rankled the priestly hierarchy were the repeated claims that Jesus had risen from the dead, for most in the Temple establishment were Sadducees, who denied any possibility of a resurrection outright.

The first blow fell during Peter's address after healing the Temple cripple. While he was still speaking, guards swarmed into Solomon's Portico, arrested the apostles, and put them into prison overnight. The next morning almost exactly the same cast assembled as that which Jesus had faced some weeks earlier. The high priest himself presided, with his father-in-law Annas and other relatives present. "By what power or by what name did you do this?" Caiaphas led off.

Peter replied with a humorous bit of irony: "If we are being examined today concerning a good deed done to a cripple . . . be it known to you all, and to all the people of Israel, that by the name of Jesus Christ of Nazareth, whom you crucified, whom God raised from the dead, by him this man is standing before you well" (4:9).

The rest of his defense pursued the same daring tack, offering a fearless testimony to the risen Christ. Pre-Pentecost Peter would have found his knees buckling before any Sanhedral collection of Jesus' enemies, but this was a new or renewed Peter. Luke explains it very simply: "Then Peter, filled with the Holy Spirit, said to them . . ." (4:8). The miracle of Pentecost was continuing.

The priests at that point must have had unhappy memories of the trial of Jesus some weeks earlier, after which there may well have been a popular backlash against the Sanhedrin for its role on Good Friday. Besides, Exhibit A was standing there, a forty-year-old lifelong cripple, who was probably flexing his newfound leg muscles from time to time in another dance or leap or kick. (Physiologically, of course, his was a double cure, since even instantly regenerated joints and sinews would have required many days' therapy to control for the first time.) In any case, the crowd knew the man had been cured, and crowds were dangerous. Thus a diplomatic solution: the Sanhedrin "charged them not to speak or teach at all in the name of Jesus" (4:18). After a few more threats the apostles were discharged.

MORE CLASHES WITH CAIAPHAS

In succeeding weeks the Christian movement only grew. The apostles had not obeyed the authorities to keep quiet about Jesus, nor had they promised they would. Caiaphas ordered them arrested again, and they were thrown into "the common prison."

This time Caiaphas assembled what must have been a major meeting of the Sanhedrin (5:21), and he summoned the prisoners before it. A much discomfited group of prison guards had to admit, red-faced and sheepish, that the captives had somehow vanished from their still-locked cells without leaving a trace. A second report to the Sanhedrists was even worse. Someone arrived to tell them: "The men whom you put in prison are standing in the Temple and teaching the people" (5:25). According to Luke, it was all due to a timely visit from "an angel of the Lord" who had opened the prison doors, the sort of intervention that Simon Peter, for one, would become almost used to.

Gingerly, the Temple police arrested the apostles once again and rather courteously escorted them into the hall of the Sanhedrin. Any violence and they would have been stoned by the crowds, with whom the Christian cause was gaining in popularity.

Caiaphas' opening statement was predictable. "We strictly charged you not to teach in this name, yet here you have filled Jerusalem with your teaching and you intend to bring this man's blood upon us."

Peter's reply has become a spiritual classic: "We must obey God rather than men," the call of conscience versus authority. Nor did he dodge the resurrection issue. "The God of our fathers raised Jesus whom you killed by hanging him on a tree. . . . And we are witnesses to these things" (5:30).

The apostles had not given an inch. Caiaphas and his colleagues were enraged enough to ponder a violent solution to the impasse. In halting a dangerous movement the ancients often eliminated not just one leader but all leaders. Amid such dark deliberations, however, a much-honored Pharisee named Gamaliel stood up and asked to speak confidentially to his colleagues. The apostles were led out.

Easily the ranking theologian of his day, Gamaliel was a

grandson of the great Rabbi Hillel, the Talmudic sage who pioneered some liberal interpretations of Hebrew law. Gamaliel continued the liberalizing tradition of his grandfather and went on to so great a career in his own right that he was the first to be honored with the title "Rabban" ("our Master") rather than the ordinary "Rabbi" ("my Master"). Since he is not mentioned in connection with Jesus' hearing before the Sanhedrin, it is not known if he was present or not. But he was very much in attendance at this later sitting of the Sanhedrin, and the chamber hushed to hear him.

"Men of Israel, take care what you do with these men," he warned. "Let them alone; for if this plan or this undertaking is of men, it will fail"—in fact, Gamaliel cited two such human failures—"but if it is of God, you will not be able to overthrow them. You might even be found opposing God!" (5:35).

Gamaliel's cool and sage advice correlates readily with the tolerant figure known so well in Jewish history. His words served to calm the Sanhedrin, which accepted his suggestion —though not completely, for the apostles received a beating before release. It was the first time since Good Friday that the Christian movement endured physical suffering. It would not be the last.

A FIRST MARTYR

As the church grew, it quickly found itself involved in matters not only spiritual but also very material. For a while the Jerusalem Christians tried a collectivistic scheme by which they deemphasized private property and "had everything in common" in order to aid their poor (4:32). Certain disadvantaged believers, especially widows, were well served by such an arrangement, but problems were inevitable.

Some Greek-speaking Jewish Christians called Hellenists felt that their widows were being slighted in the daily handouts, and they complained to the disciples. For the first time the Twelve saw the need for specialized callings in the church.

With a world to win, they could hardly abandon their efforts in the spiritual sphere, so they advised that a board of seven deacons be appointed to administer to the church's material necessities.

A man named Stephanos was one of those chosen, and his Greek name suggests that the ration for the Hellenist widows must soon have improved dramatically! At least Luke records no further complaints about the dole for charity. But Stephanos or Stephen proved to be more than a lay deacon. He was also a gifted teacher and preacher, "full of faith and of the Holy Spirit" (6:5). We wish we knew more about this man of charisma and wisdom than his brief, meteoric appearance early in the Acts account.

As with Socrates, it was Stephen's wit that got him into trouble. He took on representatives from five different synagogues in Jerusalem and debated with them at the same time, the dispute likely centering on Stephen's prediction that Christ would ultimately change Jewish customs. Stephen overpowered his opponents in debate, but, as in the case of Socrates, the losers preferred charges of impiety against him in court, in this instance, the Sanhedrin.

When Caiaphas asked this latest Christian to stand before him if the charges were justified, Stephen replied with an address which at first seems frankly disappointing, for, instead of a defense, it is a lengthy tour through Old Testament history that blurs several facts, and is surely material that members of the Sanhedrin should have known very well indeed. But early Christian preaching was heavily centered in the Old Testament—the *only* Scriptures then available, it should be remembered—and, again, the only final authority for a Jew. Stephen interpreted Israel's past as a case history of disobedience to God and a continual rejection of his prophets. This set the stage for an abrupt climax in his address, when he suddenly shifted to direct discourse:

The traditional site of the stoning of Stephen below the northeastern corner of the walls of Jerusalem above. An oratory commemorating his martyrdom is to the left, with Stephen's name in Greek lettering along its wall.

You stiff-necked people, uncircumcised in heart and ears, you always resist the Holy Spirit. As your fathers did, so do you. Which of the prophets did not your fathers persecute? And they killed those who announced beforehand the coming of the Righteous One, whom you have now betrayed and murdered, you who received the law as delivered by angels and did not keep it (7:51).

Naked rage boiled up from the ranks of the Sanhedrin, and when Stephen reported his vision of the victorious Christ in the heavens, they stopped their ears against what they deemed horrendous blasphemy. Howling with fury, the Sanhedrists did something unparalleled in Hebrew history. Members jumped up from their benches, grabbed Stephen, and dragged him out of the city to an open spot, probably just below the northeastern corner of the Temple wall. Stripping off their garments for the violent task ahead, they deposited them on the grass in front of a studious young Pharisee named Saul, who promised to look after them. Then they stooped down to pick up the commonest item on the fields of Palestine to the present day —rocks—and hurled them at Stephen until he collapsed and died.

The lynching was grossly illegal: Pontius Pilate alone had the authority to inflict capital punishment in Judea. But he had returned to his headquarters at Caesarea after the close of the Jewish Passover, and the Roman cohort of 600 auxiliaries, stationed in the nearby Tower Antonia, for some reason did not intervene. The mob action was doubtless a *fait accompli* before they could even take notice.

At the Last Supper, just before his own death, Jesus had told the Twelve: "A servant is not greater than his master. If they persecuted me, they will persecute you" (Jn. 15:20). Stephen fulfilled the prediction directly. Poignantly, he had tried to pattern his death as close to Jesus' as possible. While the stones were pounding into him, he also forgave his enemies before crying, "Lord Jesus, receive my spirit" (7:59). With that he died, the first martyr after Jesus in Christian history.

4

The Dispersion

And on that day a great persecution arose against the church in Jerusalem; and they were all scattered throughout the region of Judea and Samaria, except the apostles.

ACTS 8:1

Martyrs are protected from their future mistakes, but persecutors are not. Their errors rather compound themselves, and this earliest oppression of Christians is a classic example. Caiaphas and the authorities had evidently decided to abandon wise Gamaliel's policy and go the route of purge, persecution, and repression. But instead of eliminating Christianity they only served to spread it. Rather than nipping it in the bud, they unwittingly pruned it for healthier growth.

Saul of Tarsus, the young Pharisee who had guarded the garments of those stoning Stephen to death, now abandoned so passive a role for a far more active one. He became something of a fanatic in persecuting the Jerusalem Christians, instituting a house-by-house search for all followers of "The Way," as Christians were first identified, arresting both men and women and committing them to prison. So effective was his performance that the priests seem to have made him their chief agent for this purpose in Jerusalem, even providing him with credentials for extending the purge to Damascus.

Why was Saul so zealously anti-Christian? Had he been on the receiving end of one of Jesus' diatribes against the Pharisees and heard himself labeled a "hypocrite," "viper," or even "a

"Go into all the world and preach the gospel to the whole creation" (Mk. 16:15). A gibbous globe, photographed in 1969 by Apollo XI astronauts Armstrong, Collins, and Aldrin about 100,000 nautical miles from Earth, shows only part of the mission field Jesus had in mind. Prime targets for earliest Christianity were Asia Minor, Greece, and Italy, which project into the Mediterranean under some cloud cover at the upper left of the photograph. *(NASA)*

From the Pnyx Hill at Athens, a panorama to the east shows Mars' Hill, on the left, where Paul addressed the Athenians (Acts 17), and the Acropolis on the right, crowned with the Parthenon. *Below left* is another view of Mars' Hill from the Acropolis, looking northwestward over Athens across the agora toward the temple of Hephaestus. *Below right* are ruins of the temple of Apollo at Corinth, with the city's citadel, the Acrocorinth, in the background.

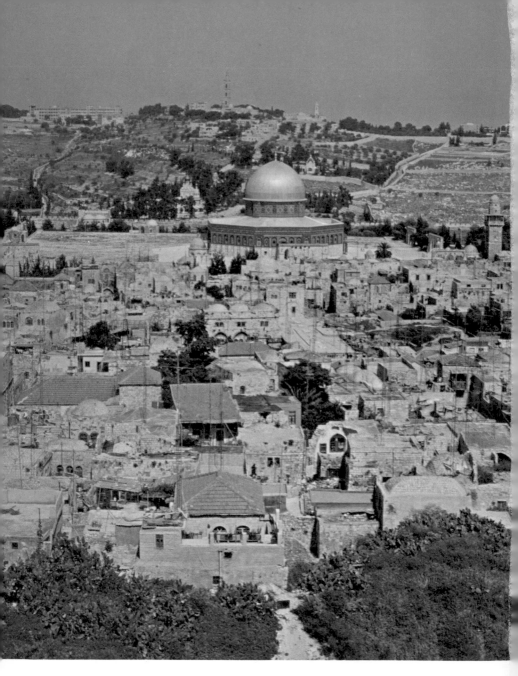

The golden Dome of the Rock (Mosque of Omar) in Jerusalem
marks the site of the Temple area and probably the Holy of Holies
itself. In the background stands the Mount of Olives, atop which the
spire of the Russian Orthodox Church of the Ascension
commemorates Jesus' departure.

whitewashed sepulcher"? No. Young Saul seems never to have met or heard Jesus personally as of that time. Was it Saul's education in Jerusalem? Again unlikely, because his prime teacher was none other than the same liberal savant, Gamaliel, who had advised a "hands-off" policy toward the apostles. For some reason such tolerance had not rubbed off on his disciple Saul, which has led critics to question whether the man who would one day be St. Paul ever had Gamaliel as his teacher, as he later claimed (22:3).

Professors, however, would be the last to admit responsibility for all the opinions and actions of their students, who hardly ever emulate them in every area. One of the items student Saul clearly did not learn at Gamaliel's feet was tolerance. The reason may be as simple as the exuberance of youth, which takes any trend or pattern laid down by the older establishment and exaggerates it. The same phenomenon that today finds young political groups at the conservative or liberal extremes would, two millennia ago, have led a young student Pharisee "educated according to the strict manner of the law of our fathers" (22:3) to outdo even the priests in his practice of orthodoxy.

The immediate effect of persecution was dispersion, not elimination, of the church in Palestine. What might have been contained to the "Greater Jerusalem" area now spread for the first time to such non-Jewish regions as Samaria and the Mediterranean coastlands. While the apostles stayed in the Holy City and served, in a sense, as board of directors to coordinate the Christian movement, most of the other believers scattered elsewhere. Exuberant about the twice-proved validity of their faith in the events of Easter and Pentecost, they could not help but become ambassadors for Christianity, and so the faith expanded. The priestly authorities had only themselves to blame.

PHILIP THE EVANGELIST

One of the most prominent of the seven deacons was another believer named Philip, not to be confused with Philip the disciple. Possessed of the same evangelistic qualities as the martyred Stephen, Philip had left his wife, four daughters, and his home in Caesarea to help launch the infant church in Jerusalem. When persecution struck, Philip answered it by accelerating efforts elsewhere. Of all places, he chose Samaria as his mission field, the home of those despised religious half-breeds who were forever the targets of Jewish disdain because of their checkered, part-Assyrian ethnic background and their departure from Hebrew orthodoxy.

Jesus, however, had ministered to the Samaritans, and so would Philip. Traveling down to an unnamed Samaritan city, he began proclaiming Christ to the multitudes who heard him there. Various clues suggest that the city was Gitta near the Plain of Sharon. Philip received an unusually warm reception from the Samaritans, and his planting of Christianity in Samaritan soil would yield one of its most important church fathers, Justin Martyr, only sixty-five years later.

Samaria was also the site of one of the strangest conversions in Christian annals. Before Philip's arrival the religious star at Gitta had been a certain Simon, a *magus* or magician who dealt in incantations, spells, astrology, necromancy, and exorcisms. Simon so impressed the credulous Samaritans that they regularly billed him as "That Power of God which is called GREAT" —a title that has escaped a truly satisfactory explanation, though scholars have surely tried. Yet when Philip announced the Good News in Samaria and confirmed it with, not magic but miracles, Simon Magus (as he came to be called) was himself so impressed that he converted and was baptized. He even seems to have become Philip's disciple, whether as genuine believer or more as "wizard's apprentice" trying to learn better magic than his own is not clear.

The holiest spot in Samaria was 3,000-foot Mt. Gerizim (the "Mount of Blessing" of Deut. 11:29), which looms over ancient Sychar. Because Pontius Pilate put down a revolt on the slopes of this hill in 36 A.D., he was recalled to Rome.

Peter and John now came down from Jerusalem in order to lay their hands on the Samaritan converts so that they might receive the Holy Spirit. When Simon Magus witnessed this, he assumed, with utter naïveté, that he might be able to purchase such powers from the apostles for cash. Offering Peter a bag of silver, he asked, "Give me also this power, that any one on whom I lay my hands may receive the Holy Spirit." It was *the* miscalculation of Simon Magus' life!

Peter's brow darkened and his eyes flashed. *"May you and your money go to hell,"* he roared, "for thinking that you can buy God's gift with money!" (8:20 TEV). Then he lectured Simon on the proper approach to the faith, concluding, "Repent therefore of this wickedness of yours, and pray to the Lord that, if possible, the intent of your heart may be forgiven you."

A much shaken Simon Magus could only stammer, "Pray for me to the Lord, that nothing of what you have said may come upon me" (8:22).

Simon seems to have remained a Christian after this episode, albeit a controversial, even heretical one. Early Christians wove him into countless legends which are difficult to unravel for the truth, if any, that they contain. The church historian Eusebius places Simon Magus among the founders of Gnostic heresy. Other sources claim he later went to Rome with an ex-prostitute named Helena and tried to fly from a huge tower there, but perished in the ensuing crash—showman to the end. Actually, the only sure thing that can be told of Simon after his clash with Peter is the extraordinary fate attending his name. One of the greatest curses in medieval Christianity was the buying and selling of church offices, termed "simony" by subsequent histories in honor of Simon Magus!

A NUBIAN TREASURER

If Simon seemed an unlikely Christian, so did the very next convert recorded in Acts. Philip, that highly mobile missionary, was now inspired to take the Good News southward on the road leading from Jerusalem to Gaza on the coast. Here, on a moving chariot, he encountered a pilgrim returning from worship at Jerusalem, reading aloud to himself from the scroll of the prophet Isaiah. Not that he was a poor reader: all ancients customarily read aloud. Luke styles the man "an Ethiopian, a eunuch, a minister of the Candace, queen of the Ethiopians, in charge of all her treasure" (8:27). In those days, however, the term Ethiopia meant the lands south of Egypt, called Nubia in ancient times and more recently the Sudan.

As to other definitions, "Candace" was the title of the Nubian queen, not her name, much as "Pharaoh" denoted the ruler of Egypt. That she should have been served by an emasculate as treasurer was common in this area of the world, ever since Potiphar of Egypt in Old Testament times, who was probably a married eunuch (Gen. 39:1). Since, however, castrates were excluded from the Israelite congregation, the Nubian was doubtless either a Gentile proselyte or a "Godfearer," the pious half-believer in Judaism (Deut. 23:1).

Philip approached his chariot to inquire, "Do you understand what you are reading?"

"How can I, unless some one guides me?" he honestly confessed. Then he showed Philip the passage from Isaiah that was bothering him:

> As a sheep led to the slaughter
> or a lamb before its shearer is dumb,
> so he opens not his mouth.
> In his humiliation justice was denied him.
> Who can describe his generation?
> For his life is taken up from the earth.

The famed Messianic prophecy from Isaiah 53, dealing with the suffering servant of the Lord, was perfect for Philip's purposes, and he used it to channel the gospel into the life of the Nubian. Together they rode across the desert, Philip instructing the treasurer all the while. Finally, they came to a spring or pool by the side of the road. "See, here is water!" the Nubian exclaimed. "What is to prevent my being baptized?" (8:37). The chariot stopped and Philip baptized the official then and there.

More is involved in this episode than the extraordinary conversion of a colorful person at a bizarre corner of Palestine. African mission work started here. The names, the places, and the connections have been lost to history, but a curiously strong Christian church developed in Nubia. Such a conversion also foreshadowed the inclusive or universal direction of the future faith in contrast to the exclusivity of its parent Judaism. People of another nation, another color, another race were clearly welcome as full members of the church, even if they were physically maimed.

Philip, meanwhile, resumed his preaching ministry via a

swing northward along the Mediterranean seacoast, beginning at Azotus—the old Philistine town formerly called Ashdod—and continuing up to his home in Caesarea. Other refugees from the Jerusalem persecution traveled even farther northward to Phoenicia; Antioch, the Syrian capital; and even the island of Cyprus (11:19). These scattered Christians were never quiet about their beliefs but shared them enthusiastically.

What began, then, as a response to persecution—dispersion of the church—served to spread Christianity in a cause generating its own momentum. But the whole expansion process, so the apostles confidently believed, was directed, inspired, and fueled by nothing less than the Spirit of Pentecost.

5

Peter the Rock

And Peter opened his mouth and said: "Truly I perceive that God shows no partiality, but in every nation any one who fears him and does what is right is acceptable to him."

ACTS 10:34–35

Simon Peter had the dual task of coordinating the Christian movement from Jerusalem and visiting the newly missionized towns and cities of Judea and Samaria. Sometimes he took on a third assignment, personally serving as missionary to open up fresh areas for the faith. So it was that he soon became "apostle to the northwest," in a sense, traveling to Lydda, Joppa, and Caesarea.

Near the southern end of the fertile Plain of Sharon stood the town of Lydda where a small Christian community was already in existence, probably deriving from Pentecost. Peter stopped there to brace up the flock and was presently brought to the bedside of a paralytic whose name was famous from Vergil's epic, Aeneas, but who had been bedridden for eight years. Stretching forth his hand, Peter said, "Aeneas, Jesus Christ heals you; rise and make your bed" (9:34). Aeneas promptly complied, astonishing the townspeople, many of whom converted. Peter's no-nonsense directive "and make your bed" was less a housekeeping suggestion and more an indication that the sickbed would no longer be needed.

Although only a modest paragraph in the Acts account, the incident provides modern travelers to the Holy Land with their first Biblical site. Lydda, called Lod today, is where Israel's international airport is located.

Two men from nearby Joppa now arrived, begging Peter to come and visit their city on the Mediterranean coast. Joppa had been the major seaport of Palestine prior to Herod's building Caesarea, and it was there that Solomon had rafts of cedar logs floated down from Lebanon and then shipped overland to Jerusalem for the construction of his Temple (2 Chron. 2:16). There, too, the prophet Jonah had tried to shirk his responsibility by taking ship to Tarshish (Jon. 1:3).

Peter had been summoned because of a crisis in the new Christian assembly there. A woman named Tabitha in Aramaic (Dorcas in Greek) had just died. She had been something of a saint-in-the-flesh, "full of good works and acts of charity." We can almost visualize her as president of the ladies' aid society at the Joppa church, or at least chief provider for the congregation's bazaars, since her friends showed Peter "tunics and other garments which Dorcas made while she was with them."

Gently, Peter escorted the mourners outside. He knelt down and prayed beside the body of the dead Dorcas. Turning to her lifeless form, he said determinedly, "Tabitha, rise." She opened her eyes, Luke reports, and sat up. Peter summoned the weeping Christians back inside the room for a glad reunion festival.

The ultimate miracle was quickly reported in the streets of Joppa, and again the wonder served far more than restoration of life to one victim, for, as an understandable result, "many believed in the Lord" (9:42). Dorcas' name would far outlast her later, second death. It lives on in the various Dorcas Societies of consecrated and gifted church women, who, like their namesake, have devoted their efforts to "good works and acts of charity."

Peter, who had now emulated his Lord even to the point of raising the dead in his name, stayed on in Joppa for some time at the Mediterranean seaside home of a man called Simon the

Traditional site of the house of Simon the Tanner at Joppa, looking northward across the Mediterranean bay.

Tanner. His name itself provides another clue to the inclusivity of the early church. Because their contact with the bodies of dead animals rendered them culticly unclean, tanners were in low repute among the Jews (Lev. 11:39). But if a castrate could become a Christian, so could a tanner. So could anyone else.

CORNELIUS THE CENTURION

The Roman governor of Palestine had only 3,000 troops with which to keep order in the land, five cohorts of 600 men each. And these soldiers were *not* of Roman stock, but auxiliary forces conscripted locally. Ordinarily, Jews might have served in such units, but they were exempted from military service because of their dietary restrictions—the Roman army moved on pork!—and in view of military action that might be required on the Sabbath. The cohorts, therefore, were usually recruited from Samaritan and Syrian mercenaries who often were less than reliable and also nourished a cordial hatred for the Jews they were supposed to police. This volatile combination caused several imbroglios during the administration of Pontius Pilate, and it could well have been Pilate himself who requested that at least one cohort of genuine Italians be sent from Rome to his capital at Caesarea for security purposes.

At any rate, the Acts account now introduces a Cornelius who was centurion in the "Italian Cohort" at Caesarea. An archaeological inscription demonstrates that there was indeed a *Cohors II Italica (civium Romanorum voluntariorum)* at Caesarea by 69 A.D., and probably earlier, a "Second Italian Cohort of Roman Citizen Volunteers." This Cornelius, while possessing a Roman family name famous since the Punic Wars, is otherwise unknown. Luke describes him as a generous, devout "God-fearer," a technical term for those Gentiles who had not become full Jewish proselytes but still worshiped the God of the Hebrews. Although uncircumcised and not bound by Jewish dietary law, Cornelius was as much interested in Judaism as was his famous counterpart in Luke's Gospel, the centurion of Capernaum who even built a synagogue for his Galilean friends (Lk. 7:5).

During a period of midafternoon prayer Cornelius was moved by a vision to send three subordinates to Joppa for a man he had never met—Simon Peter—at an address he had never known—the house of Simon the Tanner by the seaside. Peter, meanwhile, had been using Simon's house as a base for his mission work along the coast.

At noon on the day after Cornelius' vision Peter went up to the housetop to pray, feeling normal hunger pains at the time. While lunch was being prepared downstairs, he fell into a trance and saw one of the most bizarre visions this side of the Book of Revelation: a vast sheet was descending from the sky, freighted down with a Noah's ark load of animals, reptiles, and birds. A voice called out to the hungry apostle: "Rise, Peter, kill and eat."

"No, Lord," remonstrated Peter. "For I have never eaten anything that is common or unclean."

"What God has cleansed, you must not call common," the voice replied (10:13).

The same dialogue occurred twice more, after which the vision dissolved. Understandably, Peter was perplexed. Just then Cornelius' three emissaries arrived from Caesarea, at which the Spirit prompted Peter to receive them and return to Caesarea with them. When he went there and learned of Cornelius' complementary vision, the message came into focus for the apostle: Gentiles, evidently, were to receive the Good News as well, for "truly . . . God shows no partiality."

Critics have scorned the *deus ex machina* apparatus necessary to lure Peter to Caesarea, but the visions have their inner logic: nothing separated Jew and Gentile so much as dietary habits, a bone of contention time and time again in the early church, so it was no accident that the visions concerned food of the *un*kosher variety.

The episode had a glorious conclusion. Not only Cornelius was spellbound by the preaching of Peter, but so were the houseful of friends and relatives the centurion had gathered in Caesarea. Peter, too, was slowly learning his most important lesson since Pentecost. "You yourselves know how unlawful it is for a Jew to associate with or to visit any one of another nation," he confessed, which is why earliest Christianity had an almost exclusively Jewish membership. "But God has shown me that I should not call any man common or unclean." For "every one who believes in Jesus Christ receives forgiveness of sins through his name" (10:28).

Forgiveness, perhaps, but certainly *not* the preferential gift of the Holy Spirit. This would have put Jew and Gentile on the same Christian plane. But then, undoubtedly surprising the apostle himself: "While Peter was still saying this, the Holy Spirit fell on all who heard the word . . . even on the Gentiles" (10:44). The phenomenon would later be called "the Gentiles' Pentecost" because they, too, were speaking in tongues and praising God. Baptism followed, and the first Gentile clan in Palestine had been Christianized.

The remarkable event changed not only Peter but church history too. The Christian mission field would be vastly expanded from *Jews* across the world to *anyone* across the world. Other early Christians, however, would not learn the lesson as quickly as Peter. Indeed, when he returned to Jerusalem, Peter had to face acute criticism from what Acts terms "the circumcision party"—orthodox Jewish Christians—who voiced a very dietary complaint: "Why did you go to uncircumcised men and eat with them?"

Peter defended his conduct by reporting his preternatural vision in detail, and particularly the culmination at Caesarea: "As I began to speak, the Holy Spirit fell on them just as on us at the beginning."

The Jerusalem church had no choice but to applaud the tolerance of God: "Then to the Gentiles also God has granted repentance unto life" (11:3).

The miracle of Pentecost was continuing.

HEROD AGRIPPA I

Some years later Peter would face a far more serious threat, not to his theology, but to his very life itself. Judea underwent a momentous change of government in 41 A.D., when Rome withdrew her provincial governor from Caesarea and replaced him with a grandson of Herod the Great whose name was Herod Agrippa I.

The story of Agrippa's rise to power reads better than a novel, but here there is space only to report that Agrippa was a brother of the Herodias who had compassed the death of John the Baptist. After an extremely checkered career he finally attained the throne by happening to be in Rome during the critical hours when Caligula was assassinated and Claudius was hesitant to assume the emperorship. Playing a double agent's role, Agrippa firmed Claudius up in this crisis and was actually instrumental in winning the throne for him. Claudius, in turn, gratefully rewarded his friend Agrippa with nothing less than kingship in Palestine over virtually the same territory his grandfather had once ruled.

Agrippa returned to Judea in triumph and proved far more deferent to his subjects than Herod the Great had been. He had more purely Jewish blood than his grandfather, and had served the Jewish cause well some months earlier when he dissuaded Caligula from his mad scheme to erect a statue of himself inside the Temple at Jerusalem. Small wonder that Agrippa was a vastly popular ruler, and he now looked for ways to enhance his acceptance even further. How else could he assist the religious establishment in Jerusalem?

Well, the priests must have responded, there was a certain pestilential sect gaining more and more converts to the cause of that Jesus who had been crucified eight years before. And the leaders could be found right in Jerusalem.

With no Romans around to moderate his decision, Agrippa simply arrested James, the son of Zebedee, who with his brother John and Simon Peter was one of the apostolic triumvirate, the prime three who had always stood closest to Christ. There is no indication of how or why James in particular was singled out or whether he received a trial of any kind. The Acts record merely reports, somberly and bluntly, that Agrippa killed James with the sword—decapitation—just before the Passover of 41 A.D.

The second martyr for the faith had succumbed. It must have been a particularly bitter blow for Mother Zebedee, who had once asked Jesus for special places of honor for her two boys when he returned in glory.

Because Peter was the most notable Christian leader in Jerusalem, he easily became Agrippa's next target. The apostle was seized, thrown into prison at the Tower Antonia, and would have had a quick trial and execution but for the Passover which intervened. No matter, Agrippa decided, his case would be first on the docket after the festival. At this point the morale

A model of the fortress Antonia in Jerusalem, where Peter was incarcerated, is the structure to the right with four towers, just northwest of the Temple to the left. Later, Paul would be imprisoned here also. Designed by Prof. Avi-Yonah, this model is at the Holyland Hotel in Jerusalem.

of the Jerusalem Christians must have approached a nadir. With two of their prime leaders killed or imprisoned, the only recourse was "earnest prayer" not only for Peter, but for the shrouded prospects of the church itself.

In prison, meanwhile, Peter seemed almost overguarded. He had been delivered to four squads of soldiers for absolute security, sixteen men in all. At night he slept chained by the wrists to two of them *behind* the bars of his cell. There were additional guards at two stations beyond that, and finally, also, those thick walls that insulated the Antonia fortress from the rest of Jerusalem, breeched only by a huge iron gate. Why this excessive guard? Might the priests have reported to King Agrippa an earlier imprisonment of the apostle, followed by his embarrassing disappearance?

What happened is familiar since Sunday school: Peter's impossible escape the very night before Agrippa had planned to condemn him. Luke tells of the angel who apparently had more of a problem waking Peter up than causing the chains to fall from his hands or opening all the necessary prison doors, including the massive iron gate. Don't blame Peter: the man had an unbreakable habit of sleeping through crises, ever since Gethsemane. Besides, he had been subjected to so many visions lately that he could only conclude this was one more of the same. And so the angel had to walk an extra block with Peter outside the fortress to make sure the sleepy fisherman-apostle had really grasped his senses. Only then did he vanish.

Awake, finally, and understandably elated at his deliverance, Peter made for the house of John Mark in Jerusalem, the man who would one day write the earliest of the Gospels. Mark's widowed mother Mary must have been a woman of some means, because her Jerusalem town house was spacious enough to accommodate the large group of Christians who had gathered there, praying for Peter's deliverance even though by now it was midnight. She also had a maid named Rhoda, who hurried to the door when she heard it being pounded.

"Who's there?" asked Rhoda, which is Greek for "Rose."

"Simon Peter."

It *was* Peter's voice! In her delirious elation Rhoda provided one of the most human scenes in the Book of Acts. Instead of opening the door, she had to share the joy immediately or burst. Hurrying back to the conclave of Christians, she shouted, "Peter is standing at the gate!"

An immediate hushed silence, and then an opinion: "You're mad!" someone commented dryly.

"No! It's Peter. I heard him!"

"No. It's his angel. Or his spirit," another explained.

There was, however, the problem of that continual knocking. Spirits, after all, have only spiritual knuckles. The nearest Christians made a rush for the door and opened it. Would that photography had been available! The film would have shown the greathearted, kindly countenance of the big fisherman wreathed in the broadest smile his gray-bearded cheeks could muster. He had quite a story to tell.

But the next morning it was all perplexity and consternation at the palace of Herod Agrippa in west Jerusalem. The king had ordered that Peter be brought over from the Tower Antonia for trial in the same place where Jesus had stood before Pilate eight years earlier, the sprawling courtyard in front of the palace his grandfather had built. Peter, however, was nowhere to be found. Storming across the city to the Antonia, Agrippa barked questions at the helpless sentries, who could give no decent answers to the obvious queries. In a fury, Agrippa ordered that they be put to death.

Luke tacks on an amazing sequel to the scene, for he could not resist reporting what ultimately happened to Herod Agrippa I. It was some three years after this episode that Agrippa, back home in his palace at Caesarea, suffered a very strange fate. Because he had been having problems with the coastal cities of Tyre and Sidon north of him, Agrippa evidently slapped an embargo on grain shipments there from Palestine. It had the desired effect. Soon a rather hungry delegation arrived from the north country, pleading for an audience with the king so that they could sue for peace. Agrippa finally condescended to receive them. Donning his royal robes, he mounted his throne and gave the delegation so gracious an address that they shouted fawningly, "The voice of a god, and not of man!" Agrippa said nothing, though he undoubtedly smiled.

In one abrupt and violent sentence Acts concludes: "Immediately an angel of the Lord smote him, because he did not give God the glory; and he was eaten by worms and died" (12:23).

Fortunately, Josephus also reports this scene, and so the Lucan account can be supplemented with a more complete version of the grotesque episode. Agrippa's address was before a wider audience that was present in Caesarea for a festival in

The restored Roman theater at Caesarea, looking northward. It was here that King Herod Agrippa I was seized with his extraordinary illness. At the upper left is the Mediterranean.

honor of the Roman emperor. It was on the second day of these spectacles that the king entered the theater of Caesarea at daybreak to address the people, for ancients began their days with the first glimmer of dawn.

The "royal robes" Agrippa wore that morning, according to Luke, were quite a dazzling outfit, for Josephus says the garment was "woven completely of silver so that its texture was indeed wondrous." As Agrippa mounted the dais,

. . . the silver, illuminated by the touch of the first rays of the sun, was wondrously radiant and by its glitter inspired fear and awe in those who gazed intently upon it. Straightway his flatterers raised their voices from various directions—though hardly for his good— addressing him as a god. "May you be propitious to us," they added, "and if we have hitherto feared you as a man, yet henceforth we agree that you are more than mortal in your being." The king did not rebuke them nor did he reject their flattery as impious. But shortly thereafter he looked up and saw an owl perched on a rope over his head. . . .

Seven years earlier, when Agrippa had been a prisoner on Capri, an owl alighted near him. Another captive, who was a German seer, predicted that the bird would bring Agrippa good luck and release from imprisonment—which happened in fact. "But remember, when you see this owl again," the German added ominously, "your death will follow within five days."

The unnerving sight of an owl near his dais was accompanied by a stab of pain in Agrippa's heart, Josephus reports.

He was also gripped in his stomach by an ache that he felt everywhere at once and that was intense from the start. Leaping up, he said to his friends: "I, a god in your eyes, am now bidden to lay down my life. . . ." Even as he was speaking these words, he was overcome by more intense pain. They hastened, therefore, to convey him to the palace. . . . Exhausted after five straight days by the pain in his abdomen, he departed this life in the fifty-fourth year. . . .

Medical authorities have tried to diagnose Agrippa's malady, the opinions ranging from arsenic poisoning to general peritonitis following acute appendicitis, all aggravated by roundworms in the alimentary canal. Whatever the cause, it was surely an extraordinary ending to an extraordinary career.

Archaeology has added an interesting note to the story. In 1961 the Roman theater at Caesarea was excavated and partially restored. Situated along the seashore, the rising tiers of semicircular stone benches face westward toward the Mediterranean. On the dais below, a speaker would have to face eastward to address his audience and would be directly illumined by a rising sun in the early morning.

In the second century, parts of the theater were rebuilt. A two-by-three-foot stone from that reconstruction had previously stood in a public building called the "Tiberiéum" in honor of the emperor. It is cut with two-inch Latin lettering that translates: "Pontius Pilate, the Prefect of Judea, has presented the Tiberiéum [to the people of Caesarea]"—the first archaeological evidence for Agrippa's predecessor ever discovered.

A king had challenged nascent Christianity and lost—also his own kingdom, since the Romans now returned governors to Palestine. Agrippa was dead; Peter was alive. After his remarkable deliverance and the warm reunion at the house of Mark, Peter "departed and went to another place" (12:17). Where might that be? Speculation focuses on Antioch in Syria, but no one knows with any certainty, and the next chapters in Peter's life remain dim. This is because Luke has another extraordinary story to tell.

6

Saul the Fanatic

But Saul, still breathing threats and murder against the disciples
of the Lord, went to the high priest and asked him for letters to the
synagogues at Damascus, so that if he found any belonging to the
Way, men or women, he might bring them bound to Jerusalem.

ACTS 9:1–2

One of the games some historians like to play is called "Might
Have Beens," posing hypothetical alternatives to history. For
example, how different would the map of Europe look today
if Hitler had never lived? Or Napoleon? Would the Reforma-
tion have happened without a Martin Luther? And so on.

Carrying the game farther back into the past, what would
have happened to Christianity, humanly speaking, if St. Paul
had never lived? Some claim that it could never have become
a world religion, but would have remained a comparatively
small Jewish sect scattered at various places along the Mediterranean. It might have lasted a century or two, but then would
have died out entirely. Today, it is argued, only religious scholars would have known about that curious sect called "Followers
of The Way" or "Nazarenes" who worshiped a Jewish renegade prophet crucified as a common criminal by the Romans.

An overstatement? Perhaps. Christians would be the first to
insist that, with the Spirit inspiring the movement ever since
Pentecost, the spread and success of the faith were inevitable,
and that God would have tapped someone else on the shoulder
if it had not been for Paul. Still, in view of the way it actually

happened, the scenario above does point up the crucial importance of Paul of Tarsus, a man second only to Jesus himself in
the founding of Christianity.

It is very difficult to exaggerate the role of Paul in the
formation of the Christian church. The rest of the account in
Acts focuses primarily on his activities—about 60 per cent of
Luke's entire treatise—and half the New Testament books are
Paul's letters to the new congregations in the Mediterranean
world. His words are heard on a weekly basis when the epistle
lesson is read in church services, and probably more books have
been written about Paul of Tarsus than anyone else, with the
exception of Jesus of Nazareth.

One would have assumed that the greatest missionary and
theologian in the annals of the faith would surely have come
from the ranks of the Twelve. Yet how intriguing is the fact
that Paul never met Jesus personally during his public ministry,
to our knowledge. It was only *after* his transit to the spiritual
dimension that Jesus went out of his way to meet Paul, the
apostle later claimed. But the spiritual symmetry of it all shows
up clearly against the background of the first Pentecost. If this
were a celebration of God inspiring the church despite the
physical absence of Jesus, how appropriate that the greatest
convert should have come this route and gone on to change a
world as the Christ-infused man he was. But this is far ahead
of his own story.

STUDENT SAUL

Paul's original name, of course, was Saul, that of Israel's first
king, and he has already made his fanatic debut in the pages
of Acts as persecutor of the infant church. Saul's childhood is
very sketchy. He was born, not much later than Jesus himself,
in Tarsus, the capital of Cilicia, a Roman province that
wrapped itself around the northeastern corner of the Mediterranean. His family derived from the tribe of Benjamin and
were Pharisees by persuasion, which meant that young Saul

would get an excellent education in Hebrew law at home and in the synagogue. His later writings show that he was at home in at least three languages—Hebrew, Aramaic, and Greek— and in two worlds: secular Greco-Roman civilization as well as Judaism.

Saul probably had a number of brothers and sisters, but only one unnamed sister is recorded (23:16). He inherited Roman citizenship from his father, a high advantage in the ancient world, but why his family had this privilege is not known. Back in 171 B.C., in order to stimulate business, Jews were promised citizenship if they emigrated to Tarsus, and Saul's ancestors may have come with this group.

A youth spent in Tarsus had its own rewards. The city was an important cultural center where east met west, and it boasted a university second only to Athens and Alexandria. It was here that Mark Antony had first met Cleopatra a half century earlier when the Egyptian queen sailed up in her golden barge. It was here that the overland trade route to Rome stopped before traversing Asia Minor through the Taurus mountain pass, bestowing crucial commercial advantages on the city. Tarsus was a microcosm of the Mediterranean world.

Though a bright student who was destined for advanced religious study, Saul nevertheless had to learn a trade of some kind in accord with Jewish custom which prescribed some sort of craft even for scholars. The famed Rabbi Hillel was also a woodcutter, and Jesus of Nazareth a carpenter. For Saul it was tentmaking, a skill he may have learned from his father. One of the prime products for which Tarsus and its province, Cilicia, were famed was a feltlike cloth woven from goat's hair called *cilicium*. Still used today by Bedouins for their tents, *cilicium* could have been woven and sewn by Saul into cloaks, awnings, or even sails in addition to tents. His skills with this fabric would remain with him for life, rendering him economically independent.

Probably as a late teenager Saul, like so many promising

youths of the Jewish dispersion, sailed to Jerusalem to continue his studies. There he enrolled in the rabbinical school of the Pharisees, where, he later claimed, "I advanced in Judaism beyond many of my own age . . . so extremely zealous was I for the traditions of my fathers" (Gal. 1:14). We have seen how such zeal turned to fanaticism in the case of Stephen and the Christians, despite the liberal tolerance of his teacher, Gamaliel.

THE ROAD TO DAMASCUS

And now, as a postgraduate anti-Christian zealot, Saul was on his way to Damascus with credentials from the high priest for the extradition of any heretic followers of Jesus he could find in that ancient Syrian metropolis, which boasted a sizable Jewish population. The distance from Jerusalem was about 170 miles over the caravan route northward, an eight- or nine-day trip for normal travelers, but presumably less for Saul and his eager band.

About noon on the last leg of their journey, on the southern approach to Damascus, Saul suddenly staggered in his steps and fell to the ground. Ordinary sunstroke, his men might have concluded, but for the uncanny sounds they were hearing too, apparently from nowhere. Saul, however, was also blinded by a blazing light from the sky, and, as he was to repeat the story many times afterward, he heard a voice addressing him: "Saul, Saul, why do you persecute me?"

"Who are you, Lord?" he stammered. "Lord" *(Kyrie)* here meant, not Jesus, but a person with mastery and authority, which the voice obviously possessed.

"I am Jesus of Nazareth whom you are persecuting."

The horror of such a response, considering Saul's record, might have unhinged a lesser mind. Even managing a reply was an act of bravery: "What . . . what shall I do, Lord?"

"Rise, and go into Damascus, and there you will be told all that is appointed for you to do" (22:7).

The ancient Jerusalem-Damascus road, still in use, at Deraya in Syria. Here, according to local tradition, Saul received his vision of Jesus.

Throughout the momentous dialogue Saul's eyes had been shut tight in shock. Now, shakily, he got to his feet and opened his eyelids. With a ripple of new anxiety he found that he was blind. His men had to lead him by the hand into Damascus.

For the next three days Saul of Tarsus endured the greatest turmoil of his life. He hovered close to despair in his pool of darkness, unable to eat or drink. But he could still think, and his agonizing reappraisal of Jesus of Nazareth must have torn into his very soul. No one likes to learn that he is in deadly error, but when such an error takes on supernatural dimension, the implications are staggering. Saul's only recourse was prayer.

In the meantime, an equally critical dialogue was taking place between the chief Christian in Damascus, a man named Ananias, and the One who had interrupted Saul's journey. In a vision Ananias was told to go to "the street called Straight, and inquire in the house of Judas for a man of Tarsus named Saul" and heal his blindness.

Poor Ananias must have flinched in terror at the very mention of Saul's name. The first Christians seem to have had their own underground communications network, since Ananias was very well informed of Saul's activities in Jerusalem and his ominous mission to Damascus. But, according to the dialogue in Acts, "the Lord said to him, 'Go, for he is a chosen instrument of mine to carry my name before the Gentiles and kings and the sons of Israel . . .' " (9:15).

Obediently, even bravely, Ananias threaded his way through the streets of the oldest city in the world still inhabited, found Straight Street, Judas' house, and—once inside—the blinded persecutor of Christians. "Brother Saul," he said, "the Lord Jesus who appeared to you on the road by which you came, has sent me that you may regain your sight and be filled with the Holy Spirit."

Something like scales fell from Saul's eyes and he regained his sight. Then, with ebullient joy, he asked for baptism and received it. Conversion, that wonderful Latin word that means a "turning around to the other side," a "changing direction," a "whirling about," could not better characterize Saul's experience. Peter had been transformed. Now, even more dramatically, Saul was too. The miracle of Pentecost was continuing.

A few solid meals and Saul was back to normal. Some of his personality traits were not changed. His zeal and enthusiasm, for example, persisted—only in the new direction. A few days with the astonished Christians of Damascus and he was his overactive, zealous self once again, this time as a champion of Christianity, not its persecutor. Eagerly, he visited the synagogues of Damascus to proclaim variations on the message, "Jesus is the Messianic Christ, the Son of God." Shock waves registered across the Jewish community in Damascus: the man who was supposed to quarantine the followers of Jesus had become a victim of the contagion.

An underground chapel in Damascus marks the presumed site of
Ananias' home. The painting over the altar shows Saul receiving his
sight from Ananias.

EXPLANATIONS

Ever since the most celebrated conversion in history took place
it has been debated by many. Ascribing Saul's transformation
to the Christ vision or inspiration by the Spirit strikes some
critics as too exotic for belief, and they have suggested alternative explanations. Briefly, these may be grouped as follows.

Sunstroke: Saul, in this view, simply suffered some variety of
heat exhaustion and lost all composure, even sanity, until his
natural recovery, but the experience permanently warped him.
The elements alone, then, made Saul a Christian.

Admittedly, the heat in the near-desert flatlands south of
Damascus can be intense in the summertime, but sunstroke
rarely, if ever, manifests the symptoms ascribed to Saul in this
account, and recovery from it would hardly confer a drastic

change of belief. In a familiar pun, Christians *do* claim a "Son-stroke" here.

Hallucination: This perception of sights and sounds that are not actually present would be more impressive if the phenomenon had involved only Saul. His comrades, however, partially shared the experience, and group hallucination is extremely unlikely.

Epilepsy: In this view, Saul suffered a *grand mal* seizure on the road to Damascus, which warped his personality ever afterward. The main problem with this theory, however, is its overuse. Epilepsy has become a catchall explanation for problems among too many ancient personalities, including Julius Caesar, and it ought to be gracefully retired. Moreover, nearly all epileptics return to the same condition of life and belief after their seizures, which could hardly apply in Saul's case.

Psychology: Certain important predisposing factors were long preparing Saul for eventual conversion, it is argued. He was perhaps having spiritual problems with Pharisaism—much as later on Luther would be troubled by medieval theology—and his fanatic attempts to eliminate the early church only mirror these theological misgivings. Then he was confronted with apologists such as Stephen who could debate convincingly from Scripture that Jesus *was* the Messiah. Stephen's martyrdom had a further impact on him, as did that of Jesus through stories he must have heard.

Psychology may have some bearing in fact. Saul, for example, could well have been among "those from Cilicia" bested in debate with Stephen (6:9). However, something *must* have occurred on the Damascus Road that not only triggered a possible psychological preparation in the man, but also radically changed him. In the future Paul would tell and retell the story of his genuine confrontation with the living Jesus. So real was the experience in his life that he staked his entire claim to apostleship on this encounter. An apostle, by definition, had to be a witness of the risen Christ. Cheerfully, Paul could affirm that he was as much qualified by this requirement as any of the Twelve.

Traditional section of the Damascus wall from which Saul made his escape.

THE SITES TODAY

A few miles south of Damascus on the Jerusalem road a small Arab village called Deraya stands today. The place is singularly unimpressive, but the name itself is not, for Deraya means "The Vision" in Arabic. Most of the Syrian inhabitants are not sure why the village is called that, but Christians are. For it was there, according to the hoary tradition which provided the very name for the town, that Saul sustained his vision of Christ. A small Roman Catholic chapel in Deraya today memorializes that theophany.

In Damascus the "Street called Straight" is still identifiable and is still called *Darb el-Mustaqim* in Arabic, "The Straight Way," because it is the east-west *decumanus* or axis of the Roman city, as demonstrated by a triple-arched gateway at the eastern end of the street erected by the emperor Hadrian, part of which survives. Modern visitors are shown what is presumed to be the house of Judas off this thoroughfare, although its authenticity is not above question. The house of Ananias is also pointed out, and in its undercroft is a chapel dedicated to his memory.

A section of the old Damascus wall is still exhibited, even the window where the ropes were played out to lower Paul in the basket when, later on, he had to escape from the city! But this sort of precision is hardly necessary, and the entire site is doubtless not authentic.

However, the transition of Saul the Fanatic to Paul the Apostle was genuine indeed, and the course of civilization itself would reflect that transformation.

7

Paul's First Journey

The Holy Spirit said, "Set apart for me Barnabas and Saul for the work to which I have called them." Then after fasting and praying they laid their hands on them and sent them off.

ACTS 13:2–3

Much as there were silent or "hidden years" in the life of Jesus —the time he spent growing up in Nazareth—so also there were hidden years in the life of Paul—the time he spent growing up as a Christian. Between his conversion at perhaps age twenty-five and the start of his First Missionary Journey, about thirteen years elapsed. It was a period of preparation for his great mission, an interim when he had to rethink his entire theology in view of the confrontation on the Damascus Road. The Jesus who had been the object of his contempt as a false prophet was in reality the Messianic Son of God who had triumphed over death at the first Easter. The harried Christians, whom he had sought to persecute out of existence as deluded errorists, had been right the whole time. And, perhaps equally amazing to Saul, God had for some reason specifically destined him, even before he was born, to be his apostle (Gal. 1:15). It would take years of study for so total a reordering of his thought.

The first three years of this period Saul seems to have led a monastic sort of existence, probably at some oasis in the northern Arabian desert near Damascus. He may, however, also have begun mission work among the Nabataean Arabs during this interval. But at last he felt ready to make another attempt at converting the Jews of Damascus.

Like a second Stephen, Saul returned to the city of his conversion and took on all comers in debate, boldly demonstrating from Scripture that Jesus was the promised Messiah. Under these circumstances it is not surprising that a plot against Saul's life was launched, which involved also the ethnarch of the Nabataean Arabs in Damascus, since Saul was thought to be under his jurisdiction from his study sojourn in the Arabian desert. The city gates of Damascus were placed under surveillance day and night to single Saul out for some dagger thrusts.

The Christians of Damascus, however, had their own rather effective surveillance system, for they learned of the plot and the stakeouts at the gates. Late one night, in possibly the most unorthodox, yet colorful, exit staged by anyone in the Bible, they let Saul down over the city walls in a wicker basket. He then fled southward to Jerusalem.

There he met the two leading apostles, Peter, and James, the brother of Jesus, who was emerging as head of the Jerusalem church (Gal. 1:18). Saul spent fifteen days with them, during which he must have convinced them of his apostolate, while they, in astonishment at his conversion, must have related their eyewitness stories about Jesus.

Saul finally sailed back to Tarsus, where he spent the next ten years as an independent missionary in Cilicia and northern Syria (Gal. 1:21). It was a period of practical experience in preaching and teaching, an internship in which he had to learn to deal with people as well as with words. His first attempts in Damascus had been less than effective, owing possibly to his extravagant zeal. Now he was readying himself for better use as that "chosen instrument" whenever the Spirit should summon him.

The Roman gateway in the western wall of Tarsus, Saul's home town, is sometimes called "Cleopatra's Gate."

JOSEPH BARNABAS

Often, of course, the Spirit worked through people. Shortly after the first Pentecost, when the Jerusalem Christians were building a common treasury, a Jew from Cyprus named Barnabas sold some property that belonged to him and delivered the proceeds to the apostles. A sturdy, imposing figure who had the confidence of the Jerusalem church, Barnabas had helped introduce Saul in the Holy City, allaying any fears the believers there might naturally have had about the former persecutor (9:26).

Then Barnabas was sent northward to what seemed the most promising seedbed for Christianity in the Near East, the Syrian capital of Antioch. The church was growing vigorously there, since the gospel was being proclaimed to both Jews and Gentiles with astonishing results. It was in Antioch, in fact, that the faith abandoned the bulky epithet "Followers of The Way" and took on the name by which it would be known ever afterward, "Christians" (11:19).

Barnabas quickly sensed the need for more church workers in Antioch. Taking the road that wound around the corner of the Mediterranean to Tarsus, only eighty miles away, he found his friend Saul and returned with him to Antioch. For the next year Barnabas and Saul formed a teaching-preaching team in the Syrian capital, until they were required for special services elsewhere.

Luke records their summons very simply. One day, probably in 47 A.D., the Spirit told the praying believers there, "Set apart for me Barnabas and Saul for the work to which I have called them." That work turned out to be the first specially organized missionary expedition in church annals, an ideological invasion of the Greco-Roman world that aimed to announce Christianity in the heart of paganism.

It was a threesome who ultimately embarked on ship from the port of Seleucia near Antioch. Barnabas had invited his cousin, John Mark, to join the expedition, the young man at whose house Peter had stood knocking on the door after his deliverance in Jerusalem.

Like charity, mission work begins at home, and—doubtless because of Barnabas' urging—they sailed first to the island of Cyprus. Presumably they started with the opening of the sailing season on or about March 10, for strong westerlies blow later in the spring and their voyage would not have been so direct. Landing at the eastern port of Salamis, they traversed Cyprus until they reached Paphos on the west coast, the provincial capital of the island.

Cyprus was one of Rome's senatorial provinces, and at this time it was governed by a proconsul named Sergius Paulus. The governor himself met the missionary trio and inquired about their mission. Saul seems to have taken the initiative in responding, giving so eloquent a proclamation that the Roman was much impressed. But Sergius Paulus, like most heads of

These ruins mark all that remain of ancient Seleucia, the port of Antioch from which Saul and Barnabas set sail on their First Missionary Journey.

state, also had opportunists and hangers-on at his headquarters, and one of them was a *magus* named Elymas, a practitioner of the same occult crafts as Simon Magus. Fearing lest his influence over the governor slip if he converted to Christianity, Elymas interrupted Saul to oppose him.

"You *son of the Devil!*" snapped Saul in some of the strongest language recorded from his lips. "Will you not stop making crooked the straight paths of the Lord?" What particularly nettled the apostle was not only an interruption of possibly his first major Gentile conversion, but the fact that Elymas was a renegade Jew who should not have been dabbling in magic. "And now, behold, the hand of the Lord is upon you," Saul continued, "and you shall be blind and unable to see the sun for a time" (13:11).

Struck with blindness, Elymas had to be led away by others. It was the first recorded wonder from the hand of Saul, and it impressed Sergius Paulus so thoroughly that he believed the apostolic message, certainly a strategic conversion.

Although some have questioned whether or not the Roman governor actually became a convert, no one can dispute the man's existence. According to an inscription from Rome, L. Sergius Paulus was formerly a "Curator of the Banks and Beds of the Tiber," a river and flood control commissioner, most probably prior to taking up his post in Cyprus.

In reporting this incident Luke inserted his famous shift in nomenclature: "Saul, who is also called Paul" (13:9). And from here on he was called only Paul. "Paulus" was either a Roman cognomen added to his given name Saul, or, more likely, the similar-sounding name by which he preferred to be known in the future because of its familiarity to Greeks and Romans, the targets of his mission. Some scholars have suggested that Saul renamed himself in honor of his first distinguished convert, Sergius Paulus, but this seems merely coincidental.

ASIA MINOR

Their mission to Cyprus accomplished for the present, Paul, Barnabas, and Mark took ship from Paphos and sailed in a northwesterly direction to Perga on the coast of Asia Minor. There, however, the missionaries suffered some kind of personal crisis. Young Mark suddenly abandoned his colleagues and returned to Jerusalem—*why* is not stated in the New Testament.

Various suggestions have been offered involving Mark's physical health or his character—somehow, the callow youth was not able to put up with the hardships of missionary travel —but these seem less than convincing. One, hopefully fresh, surmise might be this. When the three had set out from Antioch, Barnabas appeared clearly in charge of their expedition, with Paul second in command. Yet by the time of their first landfall and, indeed, throughout the rest of the journey, Paul had plainly taken over leadership of their mission travels. John Mark, as Barnabas' cousin and friend, may have resented what he thought a usurpation of leadership by an "outsider" to the Christian cause from such "insiders" as themselves who had participated in the original Pentecost and the earliest activities of the church in Jerusalem. Whatever the cause of Mark's defection, apostles were obviously also human beings.

The first goal of Paul and Barnabas' thrust into Asia Minor was the city of Antioch in the Roman province of Galatia (not to be confused with the Syrian capital). It was no easy journey. Antioch lay about 100 miles to the north across the formidable Taurus Mountains and about 4,000 feet in altitude. It had a handsome setting in the lofty tablelands and lake district of southwestern Asia Minor, and it was also one of the most cosmopolitan communities Paul ever visited. The city boasted native Galatians, Phrygians, Greeks, Jews, and also Romans, for Antioch had recently hosted a large influx of veterans from the Roman army.

Of all these ethnic groups, however, Paul and Barnabas would first present the Good News to their own kind, a standard Pauline practice from now until the end of his mission in Rome. On the Sabbath they went into the synagogue at Antioch and sat down. They heard the standard two readings from the Law and the Prophets, and then the ruler of the synagogue extended them a cordial invitation: "Brothers, if you have any word of exhortation for the people, say it."

Paul stood up to deliver a sermonette that could not more effectively have linked Jesus to Scriptural prophecy. Like the martyred Stephen, he skimmed some of the highlights of Israel's past, but when he reached King David he moved directly to David's Messianic descendant. Jesus, Paul said, was prosecuted by Jerusalem authorities who "because they did not recognize him nor understand the utterances of the prophets which are read every sabbath, fulfilled these by condemning him" (13:27). But rejection and death were followed by resurrection and new life for Jesus as well as all believers, a prospect available also to the Jews of Antioch.

Paul's message raised a sensation in the synagogue, and he was invited back for the next Sabbath. A week later the word-of-mouth phenomenon had caused "almost the whole city" to turn out for the two missionaries. The multitudes, however, included also some representatives of Jewish orthodoxy who contradicted Paul's claims.

After what was doubtless a heated debate, Paul finally grasped what would become his cardinal alternative whenever confronted by Jewish rejection of the Christian message. Ominously, he warned:

It was necessary that the word of God should be spoken first to you. Since you thrust it from you, and judge yourselves unworthy of eternal life, behold, we turn to the Gentiles. For the Lord has commanded us, saying, "I have set you to be a light for the Gentiles, that you may bring salvation to the uttermost parts of the earth" (13:46; Is. 49:6).

There were more than enough Gentiles for a mission field in Antioch, with its crazy-quilt of different ethnic groups. It is just possible, in fact, that Paul and Barnabas had originally aimed for Antioch on the recommendation of Sergius Paulus, because archaeology has shown that the family of the governor of Cyprus had important roots in that city. With only paganism as their religious schooling, the Gentiles of Antioch gave a positive response to the Christian message, and a congregation was founded there.

Unhappily, however, increasing pressure from the synagogue finally led to outright expulsion of the two missionaries. But before leaving Antioch, they had the satisfaction of seeing their new converts "filled with joy and with the Holy Spirit" (13:52). The miracle of Pentecost was continuing.

Paul and Barnabas now headed eastward to Iconium (called Konya in modern Turkey), a city well located on a fertile fruit- and grain-producing plain. They pursued a mission pattern similar to what they had accomplished in Antioch, preaching first in the Jewish synagogue of the city. Their success here was again challenged by an orthodox Jewish reaction, which divided the city. Even though they soon had to yield to pressure and move on, the second church of Asia Minor had been founded, and it would thrive.

AN ATTEMPTED DEIFICATION

Lystra lay twenty-five miles south-southwest of Iconium, and although a sister city to Antioch in boasting a colony of Roman army veterans, it was clearly more rural and less sophisticated, if the next extraordinary scene is any indication. Paul and Barnabas had arrived in Lystra to preach the gospel, and this time Paul used a great sign to authenticate his great message. Fixing his gaze on one of his listeners who had crippled feet and had never walked in his life, he shouted, "Stand upright on your feet!" In Luke's language, the cripple "sprang up and walked."

The miracle was too much for the crowd that had gathered. Abandoning the Greek in which they and Paul had been communicating, they shouted, in their native Lycaonian tongue, "The gods have come down to us in the likeness of men!" And such gods! Barnabas they hailed as Zeus, father of the gods and men; while Paul, the chief spokesman, they called Hermes, the god of communication.

For centuries the names have led scholars to conclude that Barnabas must have had the more imposing figure and countenance of the two, with Paul smaller but more agile. It is true that *paulus* is a Latin adjective that means small or little, but it was also a common proper name in several of the great families of Rome, whose bearers were not necessarily small. More convincing are the earliest portraits of Paul in the Roman catacombs, which usually show him as a smallish figure with pointed, prying gray beard.

The acclaim at Lystra was not merely the sort of flattery

accorded King Agrippa that fateful morning in Caesarea. Those were only words. Here the bedazzled pagans went on to action. The local priest of Zeus was so sure that the chief Olympian deity had indeed arrived in Lystra, that he was processing happily up toward the gates of the temple with oxen and garlands to do public sacrifice! Lest we laugh at the naïveté of the Lystrans, it should be noted that it was in exactly this area of the world that the famous Greek myth of Baucis and Philemon had its setting. They were an aged couple who one day supposedly offered hospitality to *Zeus* and *Hermes* as they wandered by in the *likeness of men,* for which their miserable cottage was transformed into a splendid temple. Would lightning strike twice in the same area?

Paul and Barnabas quickly put an end to such speculation. Tearing their garments at the sacrilege, Paul cried, "Men, why are you doing this? We also are men, of like nature with you, and bring you good news, that you should turn from these vain things to a living God," whom he went on to describe (14:15).

Was it frustration at their misidentification that helped the crowd lend ready ears to adversaries who had just made a special trip from Antioch and Iconium to denounce the apostles? An instant, drastic change of mood swept the multitude. The gods were now imposters and must be punished. Paul was dragged outside the city by a shrieking mob and stoned to death before his supporters could save him.

Or so the Lystrans thought. Actually, Paul was doubtless knocked unconscious by one of the stones and presumed to be dead. For when Barnabas and the new believers of Lystra gathered anxiously about him, Paul regained his senses and stood up, bruised, but not mortally injured. No thoughts of self-pity swirled in his mind, for he would have been the first to remember a man named Stephen, and of how he was here receiving a slight taste of his own medicine.

The next day they left for Derbe, the last town on their itinerary, about a day's journey eastward. Here they preached without incident and "made many disciples," the first place in

Galatia where they had not encountered opposition.

From Derbe it would have been simplest for Paul and Barnabas to continue eastward through the Taurus mountain pass and home to Antioch. But what was simplest was not always best for the gospel. Since it was important to check on the progress of the new missions they had founded, the apostles went three times as far homeward in the opposite direction, bracing up the new believers in Lystra, Iconium, and Antioch, and appointing elders to guide them. This wise gesture led to permanent Christian churches in all these cities.

Finally, they returned southward to the Mediterranean coast and caught a ship bound for Syria. When Paul and Barnabas arrived in Antioch, they could deliver a very colorful missionaries' report, for God "had opened a door of faith to the Gentiles" indeed (14:27).

8

Quarrels and Controversy

But some men came down from Judea and were teaching the brethren, "Unless you are circumcised according to the custom of Moses, you cannot be saved." And . . . Paul and Barnabas had no small dissension and debate with them. . . .

ACTS 15:1–2

A certain nostalgia for early Christianity and its rapid growth rate moves many believers today. At a time when modern culture is becoming more secular than ever before and so many more babies are born than baptized, when church membership seems to be drooping and even the Sunday school is in trouble, it is small wonder that Christians are trying to revive church life by harking back to the verve and successes of the early church.

The experiences of primitive Christianity, however, can easily be overidealized; the first Pentecost was not followed by one prolonged glory story. Besides the spectacular extension of the church, Acts very honestly, very realistically, also records the instances of smallness and inconsistency among the apostles, the squabbles between the missionaries, the dishonesty and economic jealousies of some early church members, and, inevitably, the theological controversies that could rage in the church, then as now. All was hardly sweetness and light.

Shortly after the original Pentecost, for example, there was the sad story of a couple named Ananias and Sapphira. In joining the apostolic collective in Jerusalem, they had sold some of their property and pretended to give the entire proceeds from the sale to Peter, while actually withholding some of the money. For this bit of dishonesty they were both stricken and died.

Sunday school children reportedly have no trouble with this story, but many adults do, for it seems an obvious case of overpunishment. The harshness is best explained by the timing: this was just after Pentecost, during the critical birth process of the church, when the Spirit's entry into human affairs had to be taken with utter seriousness. As Peter put it, "You have not lied to men but to God" (5:4). The supernatural sign also authenticated the apostolic ministry, however severely. Still, so extremely punitive a miracle was not repeated in the early church, and one can only hope the unfortunate couple somehow found ultimate salvation, since they surely seem to have been punished enough in this life.

Other problems in the early church were economic in nature, and some, such as the Hellenist widows' complaints in Jerusalem, have been cited. A sizable number of poor Jewish Christians in Palestine seem to have been in continuing financial straits; the Jerusalem leaders mentioned their problem to Paul during one of his visits to the Holy City (Gal. 2:10), and on several occasions Paul and his associates delivered relief money to the elders there. Those with no love for socialism have suggested it was all due to the unwise collectivistic experiments of the Jerusalem Christians, but the periodic famines in the Near East may also have been a factor.

THE JERUSALEM COUNCIL

Far more significant issues, however, were now confronting the church. Among the Jerusalem Christians was a group of very strict interpreters of Jewish law—"the circumcision party" noted earlier—Christian Pharisees who were also called Judaizers. A foretaste of their theology surfaced when Peter had returned from his mission to Cornelius and they asked him,

"Why did you go to uncircumcised men and eat with them?"

Though Peter's reply satisfied them for a time, the narrow-minded legalists now dispatched representatives to Antioch, who insisted that the only way a Gentile could become a Christian was to become a Jew first: "Unless you are circumcised according to the custom of Moses, you cannot be saved" (15:1). Despite the coming of Christ, they taught, Old Testament Law still applied to Christians in its entirety.

Paul and Barnabas opposed this notion vigorously. In their journey through Asia Minor they had not required that their Gentile converts be circumcised or observe all of Jewish law, since salvation was not achievable through the Law but only through faith in Christ. Quite a debate raged in the Antioch church, since the Judaizers were calling Paul and Barnabas' entire mission enterprise into question.

The Christians of Antioch finally sent Paul, Barnabas, and Titus to Jerusalem to consult with the apostles on so basic an issue. Titus was one of Paul's Greek converts, most probably from Antioch, and he had *not* been circumcised. In other words, here was a walking, breathing test case on the theological question: was Titus a true Christian as he was, or would he have to be circumcised?

The meeting in Jerusalem was the first church council in Christian history, and its importance was categorical for the future of the faith. But for the decision it made, Christianity might not have become a world religion. Highest authorities in the church at this time were the apostles and elders who had gathered to consider the issue, with James the brother of Jesus, Peter, and John the leading three "pillars of the church."

Paul, who had been warmly received by the Jerusalem Christians, opened by giving the conclave a sample of the sort of gospel he had been preaching to the Gentiles, "lest somehow," he put it poignantly, "I should be running or had run in vain" (Gal. 2:2). If he had preached a wrong version of the faith, his fifteen years of study and missionizing would have been utterly wasted.

Panorama of Jerusalem today from the Mount of Olives. In the foreground is the Kidron Valley. At left center stands the Dome of

Paul's theology sat well with everyone but the Judaizers, who insisted adamantly, "It is necessary to circumcise the Gentiles, and to charge them to keep the law of Moses."

A drone of discussion greeted that opinion, until Simon Peter stood up and fully seconded Paul's theology. The kindly fisherman reminded the council of how God had elected also the Gentiles, "giving them the Holy Spirit just as he did to us," as witness his own special mission to Cornelius. "Now therefore," he summed up, "why do you make trial of God by putting a yoke upon the neck of the [Gentile] disciples which neither our fathers nor we have been able to bear?"

During the ensuing silence Paul and Barnabas reviewed how extraordinarily God had blessed their efforts in Asia Minor. Would he have given them power to perform wonders there if they had been preaching a wrong gospel?

the Rock, marking the site of the great Temple. To the left of this
and in the background is the location of Calvary.

James now showed his leadership of the Jerusalem church by
bringing the council to a decision. He readily sided with Peter,
Paul, and Barnabas. Arming himself with Scriptural precedent,
James announced: "Brothers . . . my judgment is that we
should not trouble those of the Gentiles who turn to God, but
should write to them to abstain from what has been sacrificed
to idols and from blood and from what is strangled and from
unchastity" (15:19).

Paul's more liberal message, then, was God's message, his
preaching authentic! Titus would not have to be circumcised,
and Gentiles could convert directly to Christianity without
going through a kind of Jewish halfway house. The four-fold
restrictions—three dietary and one moral—were very mild tok-
ens asked of the Gentiles so as not to offend their fellow Jewish
Christians. (In rabbinical tradition, the three sons of Noah,

who were thought to be progenitors of both Jews and Gentiles, had had the same restrictions placed on them.)

But the Jerusalem Council had clearly opted for salvation by faith rather than salvation by law, a momentous turn for the future of Christian theology. As Paul would later write the Galatians, ". . . we did not yield submission even for a moment [to the Judaizers], that the truth of the gospel might be preserved for you" (Gal. 2:5). Paul's victory was confirmed by a letter that the elders of the Jerusalem church wrote to the congregation in Antioch, and it was delivered by special emissaries. Paul had not run in vain. The gospel of God's free grace was Good News indeed.

SQUABBLES IN ANTIOCH

Because of Paul's evident success with the Gentiles, an almost official division of labor had been agreed upon at the close of the Jerusalem conclave: James, Peter, and John would concentrate primarily on the Jewish Christians, whereas Paul and Barnabas would specialize in Gentile mission work (Gal. 2:9). This may help explain the unhappy scene that followed soon after the council ended.

The Judaizers of Jerusalem, despite their enormous setback, were still trying to advance their cause, and a party of them returned to Antioch. Peter happened to be paying a visit to the church in Antioch at about the same time, and at first he had had no scruples about dining with the Gentile converts there. When the Judaizers showed up, however, he surrendered his table fellowship with the Gentiles to forestall any criticism from the militantly orthodox. But Peter's inconsistency grew contagious, and soon even Barnabas and other Jewish Christians were also dining on a strictly kosher basis, leaving Gentile believers by themselves . . . and justifiably offended.

Possibly Peter felt that his mission now mainly to the circumcised dictated such conduct, but it remains a sad little gesture in an otherwise noble career, a throwback to the

Simon Peter of pre-Pentecost days.

Paul quickly set Peter straight. "I opposed him to his face, because he stood condemned," Paul later wrote the Galatians. "When I saw that they were not straightforward about the truth of the gospel, I said to Cephas [Aramaic for Peter] before them all, 'If you, though a Jew, live like a Gentile and not like a Jew, how can you compel the Gentiles to live like Jews?' " (Gal. 2:11). The freedom of the gospel was at stake, and Paul would not let Peter risk it, or return to legalism.

The scene of one of the two greatest apostles castigating the other in public is extraordinary, of course, and it used to bother some of the later church fathers who tried to explain the episode away. But this is not possible.

Nor is it necessary. There is something distinctly refreshing about the realism and candor of the squabble in Antioch. Saints are sinners too, prone to failure and error, and their story is so much more believable when it is told in full. Most other biographies in the Greco-Roman world to that date are laced with fulsome flattery of their subjects and lose much credibility. The Bible, on the other hand, is the one religious book in ancient literature which admits that its heroes are sinners too, and then provides a candid look at the sins. So instead of glossing over such negatives, Acts and the epistles of Paul, with bracing honesty, report them in detail.

Another reason such scenes were included in the record may have been to comfort future generations of Christians. If, in the ruddy afterglow of the first Pentecost, the early church, informed and inflamed as it was by the Holy Spirit, could *still* become an arena of controversy between liberals and conservatives, parties and ethnic groups, then there is some small consolation for later generations of Christians which have done— and are doing—the same thing.

However, there is also a lesson from the early church on how to *solve* such controversies. The decision at the Jerusalem Council involved:

1. *A Face-to-Face Confrontation:* There was no whispering

campaign, no rush to publish, no indirect attacks or misunderstandings, but a candid exchange between reasonable men, not extremists.

2. *Listening:* Possibly the most important verse in Luke's report on the conclave is 15:12: "And all the assembly kept silence; and they listened. . . ." An honest effort was made by each side to hear the other side.

3. *A Scriptural Solution:* James based his decision on three prophets, Isaiah (45:21), Jeremiah (12:15), and Amos (9:11).

4. *Compromise:* While the word has both bad and good connotations, there is no question but that the resolution at Jerusalem, while not "compromising" (negative sense) a syllable of the gospel, still "compromised" (positive sense) by not waiving the four restrictions on Gentile Christians for the sake of harmony in the church.

Feuders-in-the-faith today might well look back to Christian origins for Christian solutions.

9

Paul's Second Journey

And after some days Paul said to Barnabas, "Come, let us return
and visit the brethren in every city where we proclaimed the word
of the Lord, and see how they are."

ACTS 15:36

The Jerusalem Council had not intended to solve all future
problems in the church. In fact, it was just after this conclave
that two "shockers" transpired: the Paul versus Peter spat in
Antioch, previously discussed, and now the Barnabas versus
Paul quarrel on whether or not John Mark should come along
on the Second Missionary Journey.

Barnabas agreed that it was time to revisit the new churches
in Galatia, but he wanted his cousin to accompany them. Paul,
however, "thought best not to take with them one who had
withdrawn from them in Pamphylia, and had not gone with
them to the work" (15:38). Was Paul being unforgiving? Or
just realistic? The kind of expeditions they were undertaking
demanded total commitment and reliability.

Barnabas refused to back down, and it actually led to a split
between the two apostles, which had doubtless been exacer-
bated by Barnabas' weakness in the face of Judaizers at Antioch. In any case, Barnabas now took Mark with him in a
separate mission journey to Cyprus, while Paul chose a new
partner named Silas, who had helped deliver the letter of
decision from the Jerusalem Council to the church in Antioch.
But good can come of evil: the net result of the apostolic

altercation was *two* missionary expeditions instead of one.

Paul and Silas started overland northward, probably first to Tarsus and then across the Taurus Mountains through the most famous pass of antiquity, the Cilician Gates. The Gates are a series of sharp defiles that notch the otherwise impregnable Taurus barrier for a distance of nearly ten miles. At one point the Gates taper down to a narrow, precipitous pass that resembles a dry gorge. Paul and Silas would undoubtedly have stopped at this spot to gather in its full significance. Here was the aorta of the ancient world through which pulsed the conquerors of the past during four thousand years of history. Hittite, Assyrian, Persian, Greek, and Roman armies had marched through that mountain gap. Xerxes, Cyrus, Xenophon, and Alexander the Great had all traversed the Cilician Gates for military conquest. Now a lonesome pair of missionaries were using the same pass for a spiritual conquest that would have far more permanent results.

Once on the higher Anatolian plateau, they turned westward to revisit the four Galatian cities Paul had missionized some months earlier and deliver to them the decision of the Jerusalem Council. At Lystra he was so impressed by a young man named Timothy, who enjoyed an excellent reputation among the Christians of the area, that he invited him to accompany them as co–worker. With a Jewish mother and a Greek father, Timothy was a personal symbol of the universality of the faith, and he accepted.

After moving on to Iconium and Antioch, the three fully intended to pass into the Roman province of Asia—roughly the western third of what is today Turkey. Instead, Paul, Silas, and Timothy found themselves heading northwestward toward the Dardanelles, "having been forbidden by the Holy Spirit to speak the word in Asia" (16:6). This passage has knitted many Christian brows, but it need not mean that God was playing favorites with the gospel. Rather, it was all a matter of timing: Paul would spend many months in Asia and its chief city, Ephesus, in the future, but for

The narrowest point of the Cilician Gates, the famous pass through the Taurus Mountains near Tarsus. Paul and Silas walked through here at the start of the Second Missionary Journey, as did a host of armies and conquerors ranging from Xerxes to Alexander.

now, the continent of Europe was waiting for their message.

On reaching the Aegean coast at Troas, very near the site of ancient Troy at the mouth of the Dardanelles, Paul dreamed one night of a Macedonian who pleaded, "Come over to Macedonia and help us." The significance of the vision was unquestioned.

"Immediately," writes Luke, "we sought to go on into Macedonia, concluding that God had called us to preach the gospel to them." Here, of course, is the celebrated "we" passage (16:10) in which Luke has shifted from the third person, leading to the conclusion that he joined the missionary trio at Troas. What Luke was doing there, where his home was, and other background details are indefinite, but that Greek Gentile physician, now a missionary and later an author, would make incalculable contributions to Christianity.

A NEW CONTINENT

The four sailed to Macedonia via the island of Samothrace and landed at the port of Neapolis, Christianity's first step onto the continent of Europe. Their objective was an important city of the area, Philippi, which lay nine miles inland across a steep mountain ridge. From the top of this rise they could easily see Philippi lying at the spur of another hill and intercepting the Via Egnatia, the main Roman highway running from Europe to Asia. And just west of the city the missionaries viewed the broad plain on which the armies of Brutus and Cassius were defeated by Antony and Octavian in avenging Caesar's assassination ninety-two years before their visit.

They broke their usual pattern at Philippi. With apparently no synagogue in town, they waited until the Sabbath and then went outside the city walls to the banks of the Gangites River about a mile west of Philippi, where there was supposed to be a gathering place of some kind for worship, possibly a synagogue. Indeed, a group of pious women did gather there, among them a wealthy businesswoman named Lydia, who was

Neapolis, where the missionaries landed in Macedonia, was Christianity's "first step in Europe." Today the port is called Kavalla.

either a Jewess or a "God-fearer." Lydia sold purple textiles. The Phoenician "patent" on dyeing fabrics in the simmering glands of the purple sea snail had now lapsed, and Asia Minor had also learned the secret of producing garments of royal purple that never faded. Lydia regularly imported these into Philippi and had a thriving business.

Paul's homily at the riverside chapel won her over to Christianity and she asked for baptism. Lydia was Paul's first European convert, and her household quickly joined her in the faith. When she prevailed upon the four missionaries to use her house as base for their ministry in Philippi, they glady accepted.

A very strange confrontation catapulted them into public attention in the city. One day as they were going to the riverside shrine, a slave girl who was a soothsayer pursued Paul and his colleagues, crying out, "These men are servants of the Most

High God, who proclaim to you the way of salvation!" Paul ignored the girl, but in the days following, each time the missionaries came upon her horizon, she shouted something similar. Her claim was accurate enough, but coming from a gypsy sort who profited from divination, it could hardly help the Christian cause in Philippi.

One day Paul lost his patience. He stopped and turned to her, addressing the spirit inside the girl: "I charge you in the name of Jesus Christ to come out of her." Immediately, the girl returned to normal—joy for her, but unhappiness for the shabby syndicate of her owners who were profiting from the girl's weird abilities. Seizing Paul and Silas, they dragged them into the central agora or market place at Philippi and indicted them before the city magistrates. "These men are Jews and they are disturbing the city," said their spokesman with anti-Semitic slurs. "They advocate customs which it is not lawful for us Romans to accept or practice" (16:20).

Romans? "Macedonian Greeks" might have been more accurate, but Philippi, like Antioch and Lystra, also had the status of a Roman colony and its official title was Colonia Augusta Julia Philippensis. And since Jews were not supposed to make converts of Roman citizens, the girl's exploiters seized on it as a convenient charge against the missionaries.

By now the ever-present downtown crowds had joined in attacking Paul and Silas, and the city magistrates—without bothering to hear a defense from the pair and against every standard of Hellenic justice—ordered the two stripped and beaten with rods. Luke and Timothy, evidently, were not with their colleagues when they healed the girl, and whether they arrived at the agora in time to see them beaten with "many blows" is not known.

Paul and Silas were thrown into the city prison, where the jailer put them in the inner keep and fastened their feet in stocks—a bit of security and a bit of torture, because stocks forced their legs apart in one cramped position. Rather than commiserate their condition, Paul and Silas started praying and

Ruins of the ancient agora or marketplace at Philippi, where Paul and
Silas were beaten.

singing cheerful hymns until midnight. Whatever catcalls may have come from the other prisoners at such a performance were soon hushed into an impressed silence.

Suddenly, a severe earthquake shook the very foundations of the jail, tearing the prisoners' chains from their anchor sockets and flinging open the doors to their cells. Somehow, the jailer had been dozing through all the singing in his keep, but he could not sleep through an earthquake. No sight was more horrifying for a warden in ancient times than open doors and an empty prison. With death the usual punishment for such laxity, the befuddled jailer drew out his dagger and opted for suicide, since, in Greco-Roman law, his widow could then inherit his estate without penalty.

"Don't harm yourself, for we're all here!" Paul shouted from the murky depths of the dungeon.

"Torches!" the jailer cried, and when light was brought, he rushed inside his prison and found it just as Paul had said. Falling down before them, he cried, "Men, what must I do to be saved?" Some have found the jailer's question a little too pat, too abrupt for such a situation, as indeed it seems. Very likely, however, the man had already had some knowledge of the sort of message Paul and Silas were bringing to Philippi.

Paul replied with what might be called the gospel-in-a-sentence: "Believe in the Lord Jesus, and you will be saved, you and your household" (16:31).

The jailer brought Paul and Silas out of prison and into his house, where he washed their wounds and fed them while Paul expounded on his original statement. Before the night was over, the elated jailer and his whole family had been baptized.

The next day the city magistrates, with uneasy conscience, sent some lictors over to release the missionaries. But Paul would have none of that. Bristling with injured innocence, he replied, "They have beaten us publicly, uncondemned, men who are Roman citizens, and have thrown us into prison; and do they now cast us out secretly? *No!* Let them come themselves and take us out!" (16:37).

Entrance to ruins of the prison at Philippi. The sign across the gate reads, in translation from the Greek: "The traditional Prison of the Apostle Paul."

Paul was not being difficult. He had his good name to clear in Philippi so that the Good News might be more credible. The city magistrates, however, trembled at the tidings: Paul had them on three counts of miscarrying justice, and the worst, certainly, was the fact that Roman citizens were *not* to be scourged or beaten. One can almost see the town fathers falling all over themselves as they personally arrived to apologize to Paul and Silas and give them V.I.P. treatment while escorting them out of prison.

Paul and his colleagues paid a final visit to the new congregation meeting at Lydia's house, and then departed after what must have been a tender good-bye. Of all the churches that he founded, Paul had a special bond with the believers at Philippi, and no congregation supported him with more genuine love, prayers, and gifts than the Philippians, as Paul's later letter to them would show. Possibly Luke had a hand in this, because he seems to have remained at Philippi for the next months to serve the new Christians there.

THE SITES TODAY

Unlike Derbe and Lystra, which at present are nothing but barren mounds blanketed by the same carpet of buff-green scrub grass that covers the Turkish plateau, Philippi boasts some impressive ruins. Fortunately, there is no modern Philippi, which means that the excavations there show the very streets and building foundations of Paul's day. The central agora or civic center where Paul and Silas were beaten is plainly visible and borders the Via Egnatia, the arterial Roman highway that the missionaries used in traveling westward after leaving the city. And in the eastern sector of the ruins at the base of a large rise, a sign in Greek hangs at the entrance to what looks like a cavern. It translates: "The traditional prison of the Apostle Paul." This site is reasonably authentic—it was the city jail—although it appears considerably smaller than would seem indicated by the account in Acts 16.

The next target city for Paul, Silas, and Timothy was Thessalonica. Even though he was called "the Apostle to the Gentiles," Paul began his ministry at Thessalonica, as he did wherever possible, in the synagogue. With Christianity resting on a Jewish foundation and calling itself "the new Israel," this was the logical place to start. For three weeks he debated Scripture in the synagogue, showing how Jesus fitted the parameters of Old Testament prophecy. Some of the Jews were persuaded, including a hospitable sort named Jason, who threw his home open to the apostles. Certain prominent Greeks of Thessalonica also joined the fledgling congregation, although Paul and his companions had to do some tentmaking in order to support themselves here (1 Thess. 2:9).

One day, when the missionaries were away, an angry crowd, fired up by opponents in the synagogue, stormed into Jason's house looking for Paul. Unable to find him, they grabbed Jason and several other believers instead, hauling them before the city magistrates with an indictment, which incidentally testified to the spread of the faith: "These men who have turned the world upside down have come here also, and Jason has received them; and they are all acting against the decrees of Caesar, saying that there is another king, Jesus" (17:6).

Pontius Pilate would have recognized the last charge, and it was disturbing enough for the civic leaders. But Jason and the other Christians posted a peace bond and were released. In order not to embarrass their host further, the missionaries slipped away by night and traveled on to Beroea. The church in Jason's house flourished, however, and Jason himself would later join Paul in Corinth (Rom. 16:21). He was another man marked by the gospel, and appropriately so, since Hellenized Jews generally chose the name Jason in Greek for their Semitic names, Joshua or Jesus.

Beroea lay about sixty miles to the west-southwest, and the synagogue there gave Paul a better hearing, for "these Jews were more noble than those in Thessalonica," according to Acts, "examining the Scriptures daily to see if these things were so" (17:11). Many in this Beroean Bible class came to the faith, but the apostolic visit was cut short again by anti-Christian agitators who now arrived from Thessalonica to stir up a riot. Paul was quickly smuggled out of Beroea and onto a ship bound for Athens, while Silas and Timothy "fronted" for him by staying a while longer in Beroea. The ruse worked.

ATHENS

Not only the chief city of Greece, then and now, Athens was also the cultural capital of the ancient world. Paul's visit there marks the first time that Christianity was announced in the heart of Mediterranean antiquity, and so the confrontation of the apostle and the Athenians is of enormous interest.

The historian finds this section of Acts particularly intriguing, and easily reacts to the text on a nearly verse-by-verse basis:

TEXT (ACTS 17)   COMMENTS

16 Now while Paul was waiting for them [Silas and Timothy] at Athens, his spirit was provoked within him as he saw that the city was full of idols. 17 So he argued in the synagogue with the Jews and the devout persons, and in the marketplace every day with those who chanced to be there. 18 Some also of the Epicurean and Stoic philosophers met him. And some said, "What would this babbler say?" Others said, "He seems to be a preacher of foreign divinities"—because he preached Jesus and the resurrection. 19 And they took hold of him and brought him to the Areopagus, saying, "May we know

Yes, the chief one, Phidias' gold-and-ivory statue of Athena, stood inside the Parthenon, 30 feet high, surrounded by satellite statuary.

Indeed, the *agora* or marketplace was the forum for this kind of exchange. It has been excavated.

Very likely, for these were the two chief philosophical schools of Hellenistic Athens, rather than the Platonists or Aristotelians.

The "babbler" would say enough to cause the erection, later, of a Greek Orthodox church over the very ruins of the *stoa poikile*, the "painted porch" where Stoicism was founded!

Greek for "Mars' Hill," a gray, rocky rise that still looms up northwest of the Athenian Acropolis.

what this new teaching is which you present? [20] For you bring some strange things to our ears; we wish to know therefore what these things mean." [21] Now all the Athenians and the (foreigners) who lived there spent their time in nothing except telling or hearing something (new.) . . .

The Greeks called them "metics," a very discerning touch here. In Athens' three-class society (citizens, metics, slaves) it was the foreigners who had vastly increased their numbers at this time.

True! Demosthenes, the great Athenian orator, tried to awaken his city to the dangers of Philip of Macedon by warning: "Are you content merely to run around asking one another, 'Is there any news today?' " (*I Philippic*, 10)

Because of the natural way in which the text correlates with Greek history, an ancient historian would have to award Luke an A for accuracy.

When they brought Paul up to the Areopagus, the Athenians also provided him with one of the most spectacular preaching stations he would ever use, for Mars' Hill still stands immediately adjacent to the great Acropolis and that diadem of classical antiquity which crowns it, the Parthenon. The gigantic gray rock that is Mars' Hill also overlooks the agora, excavated to the northwest, where Paul first encountered the philosophers. Today it is difficult to decide which is more impressive: the view of the Acropolis-Mars' Hill area from Athens below, or the panorama of Athens from atop Mars' Hill.

Paul's address to the Athenians is fascinating, for it shows the best of his sermon technique. (In his many months of future association with Paul, Luke undoubtedly learned both the thrust and the details of the speech from Paul himself.) He opens by complimenting his audience: "Men of Athens, I perceive that in every way you are very religious." In a secular age this may not rank as complimentary, but it was intended as an accolade at the time. Paul always began his addresses before Greco-Romans with marks of respect and graciousness. No practitioner of the shock method, he!

Then he mentioned having seen one of their altars inscribed:

"TO AN UNKNOWN GOD," and he used this as a brilliant opening illustration that snared their attention and led into his message. To the Athenians, who had hedged their spiritual bets by assigning an altar to placate any unknown deity, Paul now revealed his glorious *ho theos*—*The* God, the Creator, in the singular—who was a little more mature than the Athenians' deities, since God needed neither temple nor tending.

His comments in 17:26 about God creating "every race of men of one stock" (NEB) would have found a very responsive echo among his Stoic hearers, who taught something quite similar in their *Logos* concept of God. And his quotations from Epimenides and Aratus (v. 28) demonstrate that Paul of Tarsus was at home in Greek literature.

Paul also delivered a larger concept of God than is often preached or taught. The God he announced in Athens is the universal Creator who is very interested in other nations besides Israel, who is pleased to have mankind grope after him in its various halting ways, and who is an immensely understanding and forgiving God:

The times of ignorance God overlooked, but now he commands all men everywhere to repent, because he has fixed a day on which he will judge the world in righteousness by a man whom he has appointed, and of this he has given assurance to all men by raising him from the dead (17:30).

The transition to Jesus and the heart of the gospel is natural and logical: Christ is not thrust abruptly into the ears of uncomprehending hearers. No sloganeering ("Are you saved, brother?") for Paul.

At the same time, of course, the man who was never ashamed of the gospel immediately affirmed one of its stumbling blocks, the resurrection of the dead, a ridiculous notion for any sophisticated Greeks. Yet the reaction among his hearers, perhaps to Paul's surprise, was negative and yet positive too. While some mocked, others said, "We will hear you again about this."

Among those who did were Dionysius, a member of the court that sat on the Areopagus, and a woman named Damaris, Paul's first Athenian converts. Whatever became of them is not known, but today's visitor to Athens is reminded of them with crushing impact. Even if Paul may have thought his mission to Athens less than successful, Mars' Hill and the Acropolis stand at the intersection of two streets in modern Athens named "Avenue of Dionysius the Areopagite" and "St. Paul's Street." And Paul's address is engraved on a bronze plaque embedded at the base of Mars' Hill today, a place where the words of even the great Pericles are absent.

CORINTH

Paul left Athens via the Sacred Way and traveled westward along the Saronic Gulf to Corinth, the most commercial of the cities of ancient Greece. Like Troy and, later, Panama, Corinth was perfectly situated at an isthmus to control all land traffic moving north and south, as well as all sea traffic moving east and west, for before the present Corinthian Canal was cut, ships were portaged across the narrows on rolling logs.

Corinth would also be central to Paul's mission in Greece, for he stayed there eighteen months. To support himself he returned to tentmaking, and it was in this connection that he fell in with Aquila and Priscilla, a Jewish couple who worked the same trade. They had recently arrived from Rome, because the emperor Claudius had issued an edict in 49 A.D. expelling Jews from the city. Aquila and Priscilla not only soon converted to Christianity, but became close associates of Paul for the rest of his life.

Again Paul launched his mission by debating the faith in the synagogue each Sabbath day, and soon Silas arrived with Timothy to help him. As elsewhere, some believed, including Crispus, the ruler of the synagogue whom Paul baptized. But many did not, and once more the missionaries turned to the Gentiles.

A man named Titius Justus offered his home for Christian

The ruins of ancient Corinth, looking south along the Lechaion Road toward the citadel or Acrocorinth. The Jewish synagogue, Paul's Christian headquarters, and the *macellum* or meat market were all located along this street. At its southern end, the Lechaion Road meets the agora.

services in Corinth, and his premises served as Paul's headquarters for a growing mission effort over the next year and a half that saw an astonishing number of Corinthian converts. Paul himself was firmed up in his efforts here when, as Luke tells it: "The Lord said to Paul one night in a vision, 'Do not be afraid, but speak and do not be silent; for I am with you, and no man shall attack you to harm you; for I have many people in this city' " (18:9).

Perhaps understandably, the Jews of Corinth were nettled at these developments. First the ruler of their own synagogue converted to Christianity because of Paul, and then—with all the subtlety of a tidal wave—the Christians started holding services directly *next door* to their synagogue! For here is where Justus' house happened to be located, near the agora and along the Lechaion Road that led northward to the port. A Greek inscription on a block of white marble has been discovered at this spot which translates, "Synagogue of the Hebrews." And now, with the increasing number of conversions to what they deemed a heretical sect next door to them, the Jews of Corinth apprehended Paul and brought him before the tribunal.

Here, however, no mere city magistrate awaited them. Sitting on the marble platform in the center of the agora at Corinth was no less than the Roman governor of all Greece, L. Junius Gallio, officially titled "proconsul of Achaea." When Rome absorbed Greece, she made Corinth her provincial capital, and so the governor's headquarters were in this city.

The prosecution opened its case against Paul under the general theme, "This man is persuading men to worship God contrary to the law." Unquestionably, the ominous parallel was not lost on Paul: here, for the second time, a leading Christian was facing a Roman governor with the power of life and death over him. Would Gallio go Pilate's route, and he Christ's? Unlike Jesus, however, Paul would have much to say in his own defense. He opened his mouth to speak, but Gallio interrupted him.

"If it were a matter of wrongdoing or vicious crime," the governor announced, frowning at the prosecution, "I should have reason to bear with you, O Jews. But since it is a matter of questions about words and names and your own law, see to it yourselves; I refuse to be a judge of these things" (18:14). Then he threw the case out of court and cleared the area. Paul's prosecutor now received some buffeting from anti-Semites in the crowd, and although Gallio saw it, he ignored it.

A swarm of happy Christians clustered about Paul. They realized that as a Roman citizen he was not judicable under Jewish law in Corinth—it too was a Roman colony—so the apostle was free. Neither Paul nor Gallio could know it at the time, but about fifteen years after this scene, both of them would stand before the tribunal of another judge in Rome: the emperor Nero.

Anyone interested in Roman history is electrified by the

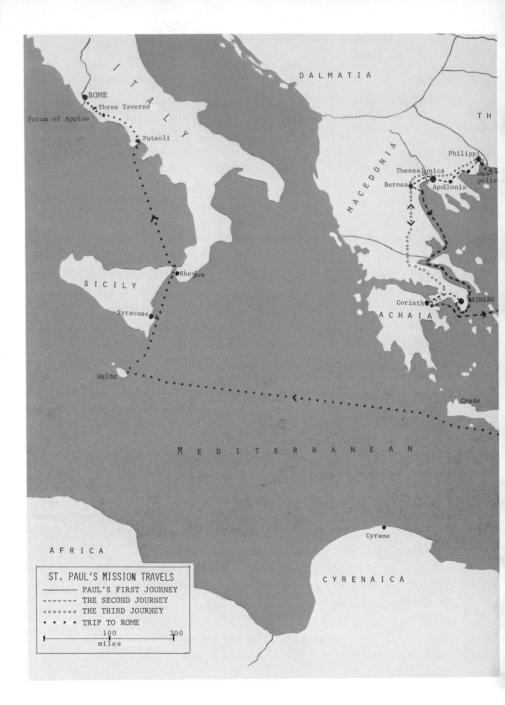

ST. PAUL'S MISSION TRAVELS
———— PAUL'S FIRST JOURNEY
- - - - - THE SECOND JOURNEY
ooooooo THE THIRD JOURNEY
• • • • TRIP TO ROME

100   200
miles

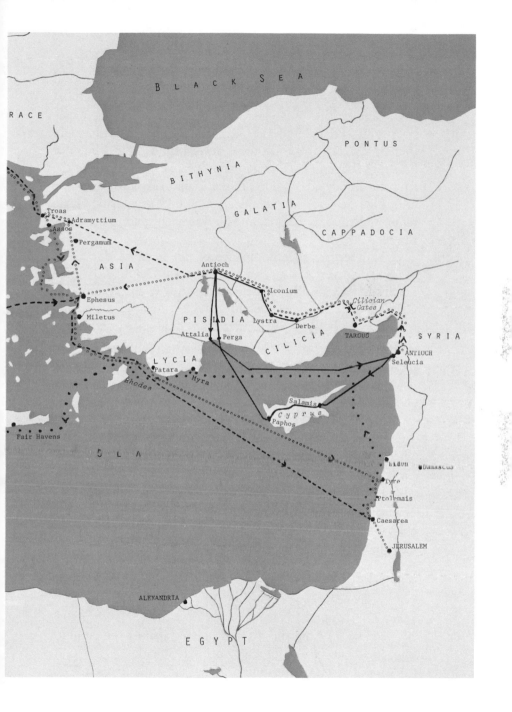

name of Lucius Junius Gallio. He may have only a "bit part" in the Book of Acts, but he is a major figure in Roman imperial history. Gallio, who hailed from Spain, was uncle of the poet Lucan and brother of Annaeus Seneca, the great Stoic philosopher who also tutored the later emperor Nero and would thereby virtually govern Rome in a short time. (The difference in names is due to Gallio's adoption by a wealthy friend of the Annaeus family, also named Junius Gallio.) According to one of brother Seneca's letters, the climate in Greece made Gallio ill, possibly due to malaria, and he was likely glad to return to Rome.

Gallio's term as governor in Greece can be dated, due to the exciting discovery of four stone fragments at Delphi, fifty miles northwest of Corinth, on which a rescript from the emperor Claudius to the city of Delphi, datable to 51–52 A.D., is inscribed. Just before the fragments are obliterated comes the significant line:

[Concerning] the present stories, and those quarrels of the citizens of which [a report has been made by Lucius] Junius Gallio, my friend, and [pro]consul [of Achaea]. . . .

This inscription has become an anchor for Pauline chronology. Because Roman proconsuls held office for only one year, or, less frequently, for two, the time of this confrontation at Corinth must have been in or about 51–52 A.D.

Gallio may have been "friend" of Claudius, but upon the emperor's death two years later, after Gallio had returned to the Senate in Rome, he coined the witty remark that if Claudius had indeed been deified, he must have been "hooked up to heaven." (Hooks were used to drag the bodies of criminals down to the Tiber.) Gallio's opinion of the next emperor, Nero, was even worse. Though for a while he served as announcer at some of Nero's spectacles, Gallio was ultimately involved with his brother in a conspiracy against the emperor and, like Seneca, was forced to commit suicide.

As does history, the stones, then, bear Luke out also. No

The *bema* or tribunal in the agora of ancient Corinth, where Paul
stood before the Roman proconsul, L. Junius Gallio.

archaeological site in the world better reflects Paul's ministry
than Corinth. Besides the marble block from the synagogue,
excavations in the middle of the southern edge of the agora
have uncovered the large marble-faced *bema* or tribunal before
which Paul stood. Aside from the Roman governor, Paul could
not have missed gazing at the Acrocorinth, a massive rock
formation that soars over the city from the south, while Gallio,
in facing northward toward the crowd, could have rested his
eyes from time to time on a background slashed with the cool
turquoise of the Gulf of Corinth.

No less than the "city manager" at Corinth—Erastus—was
converted (Rom. 16:23), and undoubtedly the stones cry out
his name too. A plaza near the theater at Corinth is paved with
limestone blocks, one of which is inscribed, in translated Latin:
"Erastus, during his aedileship, laid this pavement at his own
expense." The Latin *aedile* is easily the equivalent of the Greek

oikonomos, the "administrator" or "manager" of the city. Even the *macellum* or "meat market" Paul refers to in 1 Corinthians 10:25 is mentioned on an inscription, and it, too, seems to have stood near the church and synagogue on the Lechaion Road.

During his eighteen months in Corinth, Paul worried particularly about the new Christians in Thessalonica. But when Timothy returned from a pastoral visit there with happy news about their faith and growth, Paul wrote them a commendatory letter which also answered several questions that had been bothering them about the second coming of Christ. This letter, later known as *1 Thessalonians*, is the very earliest writing in what would one day be called the New Testament.

But just as some today are using the Book of Revelation in overliteral ways to predict the imminent return of Christ, so some of the Thessalonians had misused Paul's letter to preach that the Second Advent was in the immediate future or had already come. The apostle soon dispatched another letter northward—*2 Thessalonians*—to correct this view and counsel moderation. It seems to have had the desired effect.

By now almost three years had elapsed on the second missionary expedition, and it was high time to return to the east. Aquila and Priscilla accompanied Paul on a voyage from Cenchreae, Corinth's eastern port, as far as Ephesus, where Paul taught briefly, promising to visit the city again. Then he sailed to Caesarea and home to Antioch. It was the close of his most spectacular foray for the faith in the Mediterranean world. The seed was well planted in Europe.

10

Paul's Third Journey

While Apollos was at Corinth, Paul passed through the upper
country and came to Ephesus. There he found some disciples.

ACTS 19:1

Because Paul's activities play so predominant a role in the
second half of the Acts account, one may well wonder what was
happening meanwhile to Peter or John or Philip and the other
disciples. Though many speculations have been offered, the
plain fact is that no one knows with any certainty, since the
surviving sources are silent. Unquestionably, however, the
apostles were carrying on a missionary effort parallel to Paul's
in various directions radiating away from Jerusalem. The disciple Thomas, for example, once the risen Jesus had dispelled his
doubting, preached the Good News as far eastward as Parthia
and India, according to church traditions. Others evangelized
elsewhere.

Still others became missionaries in oblique ways, like Apollos
of Alexandria. Neither one of the Twelve nor of the Seventy
(Lk. 10:1), Apollos was a learned and eloquent Jew who converted to Christianity, but without a complete knowledge of
the faith. Nothing daunted, Apollos arrived at Ephesus and
started speaking boldly about Jesus in the synagogue there.
Listening to him in the congregation were none other than
Paul's tentmaking co–workers, Aquila and Priscilla, who invited Apollos to their home and corrected his doctrinal defect
on baptism, since Apollos "knew only the baptism of John"
(18:25).

A quick learner, Apollos was soon a fully qualified Christian missionary. Armed with letters of recommendation from the Christians of Ephesus, he now traveled to Corinth and powerfully "watered" what Paul had "planted" there (1 Cor. 3:6). Because of his specialty in relating Jesus to Hebrew Scripture, Apollos may very well have authored the epistle to the *Hebrews*, as Martin Luther surmised. Apollos, at any rate, symbolizes the dozens, perhaps hundreds of other emissaries for the faith in various parts of the Near East and the Mediterranean.

Meanwhile, after resting several months, Paul undertook yet a third mission expedition, once again taking the road northwestward from Antioch, through the Cilician Gates, and onward to the churches he had founded in Galatia. This was now the third time he visited Derbe, Lystra, Iconium, and Antioch in the "upper country" of Asia Minor, which showed their importance to Paul. Perhaps it was for this reason that the diehard Judaizers made a last, determined effort to undermine his message in these churches shortly after he left them. When Paul learned of it, he promptly wrote his most impassioned letter to the *Galatians*. After the briefest introduction, it begins:

I am astonished that you are so quickly deserting him who called you in the grace of Christ and turning to a different gospel—not that there is another gospel, but there are some who trouble you and want to pervert the gospel of Christ. But even if we, or an angel from heaven, should preach to you a gospel contrary to that which we preached to you, let him be accursed. . . . (1:6)

Following this scolding, however, Paul continued with a magnificent document that has well been called the "Magna Carta of Christian Liberty," a noble affirmation of the doctrine of justification by faith alone.

EPHESUS

In his previous journey Paul had veered northwestward to the Dardanelles, but this time he turned toward Ephesus in the southwest, the leading metropolis in the Roman province of Asia. Located three miles from the Aegean though connected to it by the Cayster River, Ephesus was a rich commercial center like Corinth, yet it also sheltered the wildest collection of pagan priests, exorcists, magicians, religious prostitutes, cultists, and charlatans in the Roman Empire. Since the great marble Temple of Artemis was the pride of Ephesus and one of the fabled Seven Wonders of the Ancient World, the city annually played host to hordes of pagan pilgrims from all over the East during the festival of Artemis in March-April. These facts were not lost on Paul of Tarsus, and his mission strategy seems clear: win for Christ in Ephesus and he could win anywhere. Ultimately, he would spend three years here, his longest sojourn in a target city thus far.

For the first three months Paul was permitted to preach his message in the synagogue, until opposition made him withdraw his converts and move over to the "hall of Tyrannus," where he would hold forth on a daily basis for the rest of his Ephesian ministry. Ancient sources do not identify this Tyrannus, but he seems to have been a Greek teacher or philosopher who owned the hall and rented it to Paul for a nominal fee. Why nominal? Because the Western manuscript of Acts adds the telling phrase that Paul taught in the hall of Tyrannus "from the fifth hour to the tenth," that is, from 11 A.M. till 4 P.M., the hottest part of the day when, presumably, Tyrannus' students had long since left the hall.

While the variant additions of the Western text are not usually favored, this one has much to commend it. The schedule would permit Paul to earn his living as tentmaker in the mornings (20:34) and still be able to preach to other citizenry and craftsmen in the afternoons when they had abandoned their own labors in the heat of the day.

His audience, in any case, must have been large, interested, and an ethnic conglomerate. There were Jews and Gentiles, Asiatics and Greeks. One early group that Paul instructed more fully were twelve followers of Apollos, who now received proper baptism and the gifts of the Spirit, including glossolalia—speaking in tongues—and prophecy. Paul himself demonstrated similar gifts in an extraordinary ministry of healing and exorcism at Ephesus, which led to a humorous story.

Ephesus was such a center for ancient magic that books on the occult arts were often styled "Ephesian writings." It was only natural, therefore, that cousins-by-profession of Simon Magus or Elymas of Cyprus should be concentrated here. Among such were seven sons of a priest named Sceva, all itinerant Jewish exorcists who were so impressed by Paul's healings in the name of Jesus that they decided to invoke that name too, merely as a magic charm and without any belief in Christ. This, in essence, remains the great difference between religion and magic: in the former, personality and faith are involved; in the latter, only forces and formulas. Gathering around a victim of demon possession in his own house, the seven sons of Sceva began their solemn exorcism, "I adjure you by the Jesus whom Paul preaches—"

"Jesus I know," the evil spirit interrupted, "and Paul I know. But *who are you?*" Instantly, the demoniac leaped on all seven, tore their clothes off, and gave them a terrible pommeling before they were able to flee the premises, bruised and naked.

One can only hope that Paul visited the powerful maniac shortly afterward to cure him, so that moderns can release their pent-up laughter at this story without seeming to make fun of the possessed. He appears to have done so in fact, because this incident was all over the streets of Ephesus before the day was out, and a hush of reverence for Paul's God blanketed the pagan metropolis.

Many practitioners of the mystical arts abruptly changed professions, gathering their magic textbooks and paraphernalia and burning them in the agora. Some red-faced Christian converts were among them, who had secretly been pursuing a parallel interest in the occult. Before the bonfire was embers, materials worth 50,000 pieces of silver (probably about $10,000) had been destroyed.

SPEAKING IN TONGUES

Paul ached to visit the new church at Corinth once again, but the opportunities in Ephesus were so obvious that he had to delay his trip there while sending Timothy on ahead of him. Shortly afterward he received disturbing reports about the Corinthians, as well as a long letter from them posing many questions about the faith. The church in Corinth, it seems, had neatly quartered itself into a Paul Faction, an Apollos, a Peter, and a Christ Faction. As if this were not enough, the Christians there were reeling under a variety of problems. One supposed convert was living in incest, others in open immorality, and still others were feuding in the pagan courts. Their letter also raised questions about food sacrificed to idols, the role of women in the church, and the nature of glossolalia and charismatic gifts.

Paul answered such queries in his incomparable documents, later called *1* and *2 Corinthians.* In a book on the first Christian Pentecost, however, it may be well to emphasize what the apostle had to say about glossolalia, for speaking in tongues is an important hallmark of the current neo-Pentecostal or charismatic movement.

The two most prominent instances of glossolalia in the New Testament, precedent-setting as they certainly became, are the Day of Pentecost (Acts 2) and the practice of the Corinthian church (1 Cor. 12–14). Clearly, two *differing* forms of glossolalia occurred on these occasions. At Pentecost three correlated phenomena appeared: a rush of wind, tongues of fire, and speaking in recognizable foreign languages, not irrational or ecstatic utterances. At the Corinthian church, on the other hand, not one of the three Pentecostal phenomena transpired. Instead, glossolalia there was of the irrational utterance variety.

To be sure, attempts have been made to equate the two instances, one school insisting it was foreign languages on both occasions, another claiming it was irrational utterances both times—but without much success. It seems obvious, however, that practitioners of glossolalia across the centuries since then—and currently—have followed the Corinthian form, unintelligible speech, *not* the experience of Pentecost.

A vivid picture of the practice at Corinth shows up in chapters 12 and 14 of Paul's first letter to the Christians there. Those who claimed the gift of tongues would stand up during services and pour out a flood of unintelligible syllables, ecstatic prose presumably inspired by the Spirit. When the glossolalia had ended, someone with the gift of interpreting tongues would translate them, if he could.

Many religious historians deem the phenomenon a carryover into the Corinthian church from pagan backgrounds, especially the Greco-Roman mystery cults in which such religious ecstasies and glossolalia were common. In this view, Paul tolerated the phenomenon at Corinth in his vast adaptability to be "all things to all men" that none be lost.

Paul, however, goes into much detail in dealing with glossolalia, and no one today should engage in the practice, or fault it, without first reading 1 Corinthians 12 and 14. The apostle does establish common ground with practitioners of tongues by claiming to have the gift himself, but he uses it only on a personal (Paul-to-God) basis, not publicly in the church, where it is patently unedifying because unintelligible (14:18).

The practice, to Paul, is certainly the least of the Spirit's gifts, offering opportunities for pride and ostentation and offense to others. He would rather speak five words plainly than utter 10,000 words in a tongue (14:19)! If everyone in the church practiced glossolalia, outsiders would consider Christians a pack of madmen (14:23). Accordingly, if tongues *had* to be used, not more than two or three were to speak, in order, and then were to wait for interpretation in each case. If no interpreter were present, silence was to prevail (14:28).

To any fair-minded reader these chapters show Paul's attitude toward glossolalia as decidedly negative on balance. Reading between his otherwise diplomatic lines, the message is clear: he would be a happy apostle if the Corinthians simply dropped the practice on any public basis, although he did not put it that badly for fear of offending any new convert.

GIFTS OF HEALING

Among the other spiritual gifts listed by Paul are "healing . . . the working of miracles" (1 Cor. 12:9). The current charismatic movement stresses these as well as glossolalia, insisting that the Spirit's miraculous gifts to the apostolic church *do* continue today exactly as they did then.

All Christians agree that the Spirit continues to bestow his gifts on the church, but they do not agree that these must be precisely the same gifts accorded the early church. Are there *no* differences between the miracles of Jesus and the apostles and the "miracles" claimed today? There certainly are, as the following table illustrates:

MIRACLES CLAIMED IN THE NEW TESTAMENT	. . . AND TODAY
People were raised from the dead.	The dead are *not* raised. (Claims of actual resurrections in Indonesia and elsewhere have been proved patently false.)

Jesus changed water into wine, walked on water, stilled tempests, and the like.

Such supernatural control over the elements of nature is not duplicated.

Miracles attempted by Jesus succeeded in each case, as also by the apostles in Acts.

Miracles attempted today do *not* succeed in so many, many instances.

Biblical miracles were attended by great restraint. Often they were performed *only* to authenticate the gospel message.

"Miracles" are lavished indiscriminately to whole audiences by many practitioners without any restraint.

The feeling of guilt was first *removed* by Jesus in most of his signs ("Your sins are forgiven"), spiritual before physical healing.

A feeling of guilt is frequently *instilled* by some current practitioners of healing. When their healing fails, the victim is often accused of not having enough faith.

Biblical miracles had permanent, positive effect.

"Miracles" claimed today sometimes result in aggravating the condition: diabetics lapsing into comas when taken off insulin, and the like.

More contrasts could be noted. This is certainly not to say that miracles *cannot* happen today. In Christian theology God never binds himself, and believers should be the very last to try restricting the Almighty. If someone has truly experienced healing, let him or her be grateful for it. But, beyond any debate, whoever insists that today's "miracles" are fully equal to those reported in the Gospels and the Book of Acts is actually *diminishing the latter.*

The New Testament miracles were necessary to authenticate the message of Jesus and the disciples and to assist the spread of Christianity. But when, after the apostolic age, the faith was broadly established in the Mediterranean world, the great miracles seem to have ceased on any regular basis.

God, evidently, did not feel obliged to keep supplying believers with supernatural proof after supernatural proof, necessary as these were in the first century to help launch the faith.

Meanwhile, one of the most dramatic scenes in all of Paul's travels was unfolding at Ephesus. A silversmith named Demetrius was making his fortune by manufacturing statuettes of the goddess Artemis and miniature silver models of her temple in Ephesus—much like the tourist trinkets still available at that Turkish site today. But business had been falling off in a strangely direct proportion to Paul's mission successes. The relationship was not lost on Demetrius.

Calling a meeting of all craftsmen and jobbers in the Ephesian metalworking guild, Demetrius delivered an emotional harangue, warning that Paul had tainted both Ephesus and most of the province of Asia with the perfectly awful opinion that "gods made with hands are not gods" (19:26).—A better slogan Paul could not have devised!—Demetrius continued:

And there is danger not only that this trade of ours may come into disrepute but also that the temple of the great goddess Artemis may count for nothing, and that she may even be deposed from her magnificence, she whom all Asia and the world worship (19:27).

Their profits threatened, the angry craftsmen started shouting, *"Great is Artemis of the Ephesians!"* Pouring into the street, they kindled a demonstration by yelling at all the citizenry, "To the theater!" A general confusion ensued, in which many of the townspeople rushed over to their massive 24,000-seat theater carved into the side of a mountain looming up from Ephesus.

Two of Paul's companions in travel, Macedonians named Gaius and Aristarchus, were discovered by the silversmiths and dragged into the theater also. When he learned of it, Paul

Artemis (Diana) of Ephesus as the multibreasted fertility goddess of Asia Minor. This marble statue stands in the museum at Ephesus in Turkey.

wanted to go there too, but the Christians of Ephesus wisely prevented that, as did a timely message from some of his friends among the "Asiarchs" of the city, who warned him not to venture outside. The Asiarchs were Roman officials whose duty it was to advance the emperor's cult and supervise his festivals in the provinces. Doubtless they were friendly to Paul, because he had finally broken Artemis' religious monopoly in Ephesus, something they had been trying to do for years.

Over at the theater a full-dress riot was brewing. The Ephesian Jews prompted one of their number, Alexander, to stand up in the orchestra and make it clear to the crowd that Paul did not represent them. Alexander raised his hands for silence. Then someone yelled that he was a Jew, and bedlam broke out. Most of the theater started chanting, *"Great is Artemis of the Ephesians!"*

The craftsmen were nearly as suspicious of Jews as of Christians, for Jews, too, taught that "gods made with hands are not gods," and they were known to disrupt pagan shrines.

"GREAT IS ARTEMIS OF THE EPHESIANS!" The shouts, now as synchronized and rhythmic as a cheering section at an athletic event, went on for no less than two hours. "Great" she was indeed, that versatile deity of Ephesus. Originally a local fertility goddess like the Phoenician Astarte, the Greeks claimed her as Artemis and the Romans as Diana, though all surviving statues in the area show her cluttered with many breasts as the fecundity figure she originally was, rather than the more refined Diana who was twin sister to Apollo and moon goddess in Greco-Roman mythology.

The highest magistrate available in Ephesus during the riot was the city clerk, who soon arrived and quickly quieted the crowd. "Men of Ephesus," he cried, "everyone *knows* that our city is temple keeper of the great Artemis, and of the sacred stone that fell from the sky [probably a meteorite that fell in Galatia, sacred to Cybele]. Since these facts are beyond debate, you should be quiet and do nothing rash against these innocent men!" Continuing, in Luke's words:

> If therefore Demetrius and the craftsmen with him have a complaint against any one, the courts are open, and there are proconsuls; let them bring charges against one another. But if you seek anything further, it shall be settled in the regular assembly. For we are in danger of being charged with rioting today, there being no cause that we can give to justify this commotion (19:38).

With that he dismissed the crowds. Too tired and too hoarse to challenge him further, the throng dispersed.

Moderns can sit in the very seats so vacated, for the great theater at Ephesus has finally been fully excavated, a magnificent structure in three vast tiers of semicircular marble seats on which the audience faced westward to view the waterfront. Perhaps the most beautiful boulevard of antiquity, the Arcadian Way, connected the theater with the port of Ephesus, and its pavement still shows cruciform grafitti cut by some early Christians there. No one can sit in any of the 24,000 empty seats today and fail to hear a speaker plainly in the orchestra below . . . and perhaps also the faint echo of a crowd chanting, "Great is Artemis of the Ephesians!"

The Arcadian Way at ancient Ephesus looking eastward toward the great theater, carved into the side of the mountain overlooking the city.

A LAST VISIT TO GREECE

Soon after the riot Paul took his leave of the believers in Ephesus and traveled to Greece via Macedonia. Quite naturally he had to see if conditions had improved in Corinth, and he stayed there for three months during the winter of 56 A.D. He had also been tending a pet project over the previous months. To symbolize the unity of Jewish and Gentile Christians and to show to the believers in Palestine the concern their Gentile brothers felt for them, Paul was collecting contributions from all the Gentile churches on his itinerary for the needy Jerusalem Christians. Such gifts might also put to rest any suspicions the church there might have had about his ministry.

At Corinth he also wrote his longest and most theological

View from the top of the 24,000-seat theater at Ephesus, where the silversmiths' riot against St. Paul occurred (Acts 19). At upper right is the Arcadian Way.

epistle, the powerful letter to the *Romans,* which relates law and gospel more fully than he had ever done previously. He also told the Christians in Rome of his plans for a future visit to the western Mediterranean world, including Rome and even Spain.

But now it was time to take his collection to Jerusalem. A sea voyage would have been quickest, but when a plot against him was discovered—possibly involving sabotage of the ship—Paul shifted his plans and returned overland instead. This also gave him the opportunity of revisiting the new churches in Beroea, Thessalonica, and Philippi accompanied by what was now a total of eight co–workers including Luke, who seems to have rejoined the missionary band at Philippi and would stay at Paul's side from this point on (20:4).

They spent a week along the Dardanelles in Troas, and on

the night before their departure Paul still had so much to tell the Christians there that he actually talked on till midnight. They were meeting in an upper room, where many burning oil lamps warmed the atmosphere and made at least one member of the congregation very sleepy, a young man named Eutychus. Even if his name meant "Fortunate" in Greek, Eutychus was not so lucky. Falling asleep, he dropped out of the third-story window where he had been sitting onto the ground below. Though he was "taken up dead" by the crowd, Paul bent over the youth and said, "Do not be alarmed, for his life is in him." And so it was, for he soon revived. Whether this was a case of concussion or resurrection is not clear in the Acts text. But the happy congregation now broke out the food, after which Paul and the flock conversed until daybreak.

The missionary band then set sail southward along the coast of Asia Minor to the port of Miletus. There Paul sent word to the elders of the church at Ephesus to come meet him for a final good-bye, final because Paul now had premonitions that this would be his last journey to that area: "The Holy Spirit testifies to me in every city that imprisonment and afflictions await me. . . . you will see my face no more" (20:23).

His manner, however, was not lugubrious. He rather gave the Ephesian elders a bracing little course in church administration: "Take heed to yourselves and to all the flock, in which the Holy Spirit has made you overseers, to care for the church of God which he obtained with the blood of his own Son" (20:28). After a final prayer together, and weeping embraces, they saw Paul off to his ship.

Sailing across the eastern Mediterranean, they landed at the port of Tyre, Paul's first visit to Phoenicia, but already a Christian congregation was thriving in that city, which had heard enough about the apostle to love him and also warn him of difficulties to be expected in Jerusalem. Paul dismissed the warning, because he wanted to take his collection to the Holy City by Pentecost if possible. Thence they sailed to Caesarea, where they spent some time at the home of the same Philip who had opened a mission thrust to Samaria. Two great apostles had been reunited. The church's outreach had come full circle.

11

Jeopardy in Jerusalem

"What are you doing, weeping and breaking my heart? For I am ready not only to be imprisoned but even to die at Jerusalem for the name of the Lord Jesus."

ACTS 21:13

Thus Paul addressed his friends in the house of Philip. A prophet named Agabus had arrived at Caesarea and performed a symbolic act on Paul. Taking the apostle's belt, he had bound his hands and feet, warning: "So shall the Jews at Jerusalem bind the man who owns this girdle and deliver him into the hands of the Gentiles."

Paul, however, would not be deterred. When the missionaries reached Jerusalem, they visited James and the elders of the church, delivering to them the Gentile collection. It was there, rather than Antioch, that Paul reported on his third expedition, and the leaders of the Jerusalem church were thrilled by his account. They also told Paul of "many thousands" of Jewish Christian converts in Palestine.

In that group, however, there was a problem. Some of its more legalistic members, the Judaizers, were still carrying on their campaign against Paul, this time charging that in his mission work the apostle was telling not only Gentiles but also Jews to "forsake Moses" and refrain from circumcising their children. The charge was untrue—the church leaders knew that—so they proposed that Paul publicly observe Hebrew law by paying for the Temple sacrifices of four Jewish Christians

118

who had taken a Nazirite vow (Num. 6) and purify himself with them.

Diplomatically, Paul agreed. He surely had better things to do, but he went through the week-long ritual at the Temple and had nearly finished it when disaster struck. A group of Jewish pilgrims from Ephesus suddenly recognized Paul in the Temple precincts and grabbed him.

"Men of Israel, help!" they shouted, and then identified Paul as a teacher who attacked the Jews, the Law, and the Temple everywhere he could. "Moreover," they added ominously, "he also brought Greeks into the Temple, and he has defiled this holy place" (21:28). The last was a lethal charge. Marking off an inner enclosure in the Temple were thirteen stele—stone slabs—that bore the following inscription in Hebrew and Greek:

> Let no Gentile enter within the balustrade and enclosure surrounding the sanctuary. Whoever is caught will be personally responsible for his consequent death.

Two of these notices have been discovered; one is still intact. Later on the Roman conqueror Titus would attest to the power of these signs when he told some Jerusalemites, "Have we not given you permission to put to death any who pass beyond [these notices], even if he were a Roman?"

Here, then, was one Roman Jew from Tarsus whom the enraged crowd that had gathered would dispose of in short order. Paul was dragged out of the Temple and was well on his way to getting stoned to death while he doubtless protested that it was all a dreadful mistake. Previously, his accusers had seen him in Jerusalem with an Ephesian Gentile, one Trophimus, yet he had *not* accompanied Paul inside the Temple as they had supposed. But try to argue with a mob.

Fortunately for Paul, the Roman cohort of Jerusalem was stationed in the Tower Antonia, which overlooked the entire

For a presumed violation of the warning on this stone slab, Paul was arrested in Jerusalem. One of thirteen such signs surrounding the inner Temple area, it threatened death to any Gentile who walked into the sacred precincts. The Greek term for "death," *thanaton,* is the last word on this inscription, which is now at the Archaeological Museum in Istanbul.

Temple precinct from its northwestern corner. The uproar brought the Roman tribune and his troops running out of the Antonia and over to Paul, whom they arrested and chained. Because the throng now pressed in on every side, yelling, *"Away with him!"* Paul actually had to be carried up the steps in front of the fortress.

Just before they moved inside the gate, Paul spoke to the tribune in Greek. This surprised the commander, since he had assumed Paul was a troublemaking pseudoprophet from Egypt who had previously led 4,000 men out of the desert to attack Jerusalem. (Josephus also reports the episode, though with less restraint than Luke he sets the number of rebels as an improbably high 30,000.) Paul quickly set the tribune straight and then begged permission to address the crowd. Permission was granted.

Using the staircase at the Antonia as his pulpit, Paul delivered his message with passionate honesty, beginning with his background at Tarsus and his education under Gamaliel, and continuing in detail with his conversion experience on the Damascus Road. He next reported a theophany while praying at the Jerusalem Temple, in which Jesus warned him to flee the city and testify instead to the Gentiles.

The last was too much for the crowd. They stopped listening and started yelling: *"Away with such a fellow from the earth!"* *"He shouldn't go on living!"* Some were throwing handfuls of dust into the air, while others waved their garments in what was now an out-and-out riot.

The tribune immediately ordered Paul inside the Antonia and had him stripped for scourging. With so much shouting the man must have been guilty of something, and a little lashing would bring a confession out of him. Coolly, Paul waited until they had tied him up with thongs before he asked a question with all the innocence of a Roman battering-ram: "Is it lawful for you to scourge a man who is a Roman citizen? And uncondemned?"

Astonished and embarrassed, the tribune corroborated the claim of citizenship with Paul before he stated, "I bought my citizenship for a large sum." His Greek name, Claudius Lysias, showed that purchase was necessary.

"But I was *born* a citizen," Paul could reply proudly. Instantly, he was untied.

BEFORE THE SANHEDRIN

Lysias still had to have an explanation for the riot, so he convened a meeting of the Jewish Sanhedrin the next morning and brought Paul before it, not to try him but to discover the basis of the furore. The hearing got off to a very bad start. Paul began: "Brethren, I have lived before God in all good conscience up to this day—"

"*Strike him on the mouth!*" someone shouted from the marble benches.

"God shall strike *you*, you whitewashed wall!" cried Paul, glaring in fury at the figure. "Are you sitting to judge me according to the law, and yet contrary to the law you order me to be struck?"

Some bystanders now identified Paul's antagonist. "Would you revile God's *high priest?*" they asked.

Paul lowered his voice and replied, "I did not know, brethren, that he was the high priest; for it is written, 'You shall not speak evil of a ruler of your people' " (23:5).

High priest at the time was Ananias Ben-Nebedeus, and his unwarranted, arbitrary conduct here correlates well with the cruel streak in his character known from purely Jewish sources. Ananias would later be hunted down and killed by Jewish rebels when they found him hiding in an aqueduct at the start of their war with Rome.

As with other speeches in Acts, Luke has not necessarily provided complete transcripts, and Paul probably went on with a lengthy defense until he was either shouted down or saw a dangerous potential developing in the Sanhedrin. For now he rather cleverly extricated himself by crying, "Brothers, I am a Pharisee, a son of Pharisees, and it is concerning the resurrection of the dead that I am on trial."

This immediately set the chamber to quarreling, because the majority party in the Sanhedrin were Sadducees, who rejected any resurrection, or angel or spirit, whereas the Pharisees upheld them all and would now serve as at least temporary allies of Paul while the two parties squared off in theological combat. Soon the debate reached the physical level, and the tribune ordered Paul removed for safety.

The episode is refreshing. It shows Paul as a very human sort, who was not above using tricks and ploys to get himself out of a scrape if necessary. A larger-than-life saint of God might well have taken a passive, resigned stance before the Sanhedrin. Not Paul.

During his next day or two at the Antonia fortress, things went well for Paul, who was more under detention than imprisonment. He also experienced another reassuring theophany, which predicted, "You must bear witness also at Rome" (23:11). But then his young nephew visited him with some alarming news. Paul thought only a moment before telling the lad to carry his information to Lysias.

It was nothing less than a plot on Paul's life. The tribune would be asked to send Paul back to the Sanhedrin for further questioning. "But do not yield to them," the youth begged Lysias, "for more than forty of their men lie in ambush for him, having bound themselves by an oath neither to eat nor drink till they have killed him."

The tribune's brow wrinkled as he replied to Paul's nephew, "Tell no one that you have informed me of this." Summoning two centurions, he ordered them to prepare a guard for about 9 P.M. that night to conduct Paul safely to Felix, the provincial governor in Caesarea. Two hundred soldiers would be needed, again as many spearmen, and seventy cavalry. The size of such a guard is astonishing, although if Paul had been discovered within the city and a riot broken out, all 470 men would have been kept busy enough protecting their prisoner—and themselves.

Everything worked as planned. Paul was given a mount to ride, and when they reached the Plain of Sharon safely, only the seventy horse continued with him to Caesarea. The rest of the guard returned to Jerusalem.

Upon arrival at Caesarea the guard brought Paul before Felix and handed the governor a letter from Lysias, detailing the circumstances of Paul's arrest. The letter went on, accurately enough:

I found that he was accused about questions of their law, but charged with nothing deserving death or imprisonment. And when it was disclosed to me that there would be a plot against the man, I sent him to you at once, ordering his accusers also to state before you what they have against him (23:29).

During the five days that intervened between Paul's arrival and that of his accusers, the apostle was kept under guard in Herod's palace at Caesarea, where Pontius Pilate had lived and Herod Agrippa had spent his last days.

ANTONIUS FELIX

Like Gallio—Paul's judge in Corinth, Felix—his judge in Caesarea—is very well known in Roman sources. His rise to power as procurator of Judea (for so the governors were now styled) was from the very bottom of Roman society. Felix and his brother Pallas had been slaves who had somehow won their freedom and were later both appointed to high posts by Claudius. Pallas, in carrying a secret message to Capri, had once averted disaster for the emperor Tiberius by alerting him to a conspiracy against him. Serving subsequently as Claudius' finance minister, Pallas became one of the richest and most powerful men in all the Empire, and it was doubtless due to his influence that brother Felix was appointed as governor of Judea in 52 A.D.

For his part, Felix had been marrying repeatedly, but well. In all he wed three women of royalty: one wife is unknown, another was granddaughter of Antony and Cleopatra, and his current spouse was a beautiful Jewess named Drusilla, a daughter of Herod Agrippa I. With his powerful connections in Rome, however, Felix felt he could conduct a government of extortion, cruelty, and oppression in Palestine with impunity, as even the Roman Tacitus admits in pointing to Felix as prime cause of the great Jewish rebellion against Rome in 66 A.D.

Such was the man who sat on his tribunal before Paul and his accusers, who had now arrived from Jerusalem. They included the high priest himself and some of the members of the Sanhedrin. When Felix called for the accusation, a spokesman for the prosecution, one Tertullus, arose and flattered the governor with a flowery, saccharine introduction that was laughably false, though true to Roman court procedure. Then Tertullus lodged his formal indictment of Paul:

We have found this man a pestilent fellow, an agitator among all the Jews throughout the world, and a ringleader of the sect of the Nazarenes. He even tried to profane the temple, but we seized him. By examining him yourself you will be able to learn from him about everything of which we accuse him (24:5).

The Sanhedrists seconded his charges against Paul, supplying whatever evidence they could.

Next Felix called for the defense. With a far less flattering introduction, Paul took on all three charges and disposed of them as follows:

1. *A pestilent agitator?* In Jerusalem, "they did not find me disputing with any one or stirring up a crowd, either in the temple or in the synagogues, or in the city."
2. *A ringleader of the Nazarenes?* In effect: Yes, but so what. As Paul put it: "According to the Way, which they call a sect, I worship the God of our fathers, believing everything laid down by the law or written in the prophets, having a hope in God which these themselves accept, that there will be a resurrection of both the just and the unjust." Thus Paul's thesis here and everywhere: Christianity was the fulfillment of Judaism.
3. *Profaner of the Temple?* This, of course, would be the easiest charge to disprove, and doubtless Paul had, or would soon get, a deposition from Trophimus that he had *not* set foot in the sacred precincts. Paul affirmed that he was merely on a charitable mission to Jerusalem and observing the Temple rites when he was attacked by some pilgrims from Ephesus who "ought to be here before you to make an accusation if they have anything against me" (24:10).

Paul, who knew his Roman law, was eminently correct on the last point.

Having heard the evidence, Felix pondered the case. Since he had "a rather accurate knowledge of the Way," as Luke states, he probably realized that the religious dimension of the quarrel was beyond his jurisdiction. But if he simply released Paul, he would further antagonize the Jewish authorities, who likely were building a brief against him for maladministration. On the other hand, he could not sentence Paul for any political or criminal act. Nor could he abandon him to the Sanhedrin, because he was a Roman citizen.

And so . . . no decision. Felix merely stalled, telling the prosecution he would decide the case in the future. Meanwhile, he left Paul under loose confinement with some liberties, including unrestricted access to friends. But there was something about the apostle that intrigued the governor, and he sent for him repeatedly in months to come. Once he had Paul speak in the presence of his wife Drusilla, too. Knowing Felix' true character, his response according to Acts is almost humorous: when Paul held forth on "justice and self-control and future judgment, Felix was alarmed and said, 'Go away for the present' . . ." (24:25). If truth were told, Felix wanted nothing more than a big bribe to release his prisoner, which was quite in character for the governor.

For the next two years Paul was in confinement at Caesarea because of this impasse. Felix, "desiring to do the Jews a favor," kept him so, but the time was not lost. Paul was busy with his letters to the churches. And it was during these months that Luke most likely visited Jerusalem to learn from the elders there all the many facts about Jesus which the gifted Greek would later work into the Gospel bearing his name. He must also have had special interviews with Mary, the mother of Jesus, who was presumably staying with John at Jerusalem. This would explain Luke's crucial portrayal of the Christmas story, details that only Mary would know.

APPEAL TO CAESAR

About 58 A.D. Felix was recalled by the emperor Nero, and a delegation of Jews lost no time in sailing to Rome to indict the

Ruins of a jetty at ancient Caesarea, the Mediterranean port and
Roman capital of Palestine, where Paul was imprisoned for two years.

ex-governor for maladministration. His brother Pallas, however, had enough influence with Nero, even in retirement, to have the charges quashed. After this, Felix and his wife drop out of history, and only their son and daughter-in-law are cited, a luckless couple who died during the famous eruption of Mt. Vesuvius in 79 A.D.

The new governor sent to Palestine was Porcius Festus, certainly an improvement on Felix. Quite diplomatically, Festus spent his first days at the religious, not political capital of Judea, Jerusalem. When the priests mentioned Paul's case to him, he invited them to return with him to Caesarea and renew their charges.

They accepted the suggestion, and Paul soon had a second formal hearing. It was much like the first, except that the prosecution seemed to have even less evidence after the two-year lapse. Besides, the high priest Ananias was deposed about this time, so the charges against Paul were tenuous at best. Had Festus been firmly in office for some months, he would doubtless have released Paul. But he was a neophyte, quite anxious to please his new subjects and still treat Paul fairly. He thought he had the perfect solution in an ingenuous suggestion for Paul: "Are you willing to go up to Jerusalem and stand trial on these charges before me there?" (25:9 NEB)

"Twenty-four months in confinement for *this?*" Paul must have thought, struggling to keep his temper under control. His next statement would change his life irrevocably, and he uttered it with passion:

I am standing before Caesar's tribunal, where I ought to be tried; to the Jews I have done no wrong, as you know very well. If then I am a wrongdoer, and have committed anything for which I deserve to die, I do not seek to escape death. But if there is nothing in their charges against me, no one can give me up to them. *I appeal to Caesar.*

It was his right as a Roman citizen. Festus immediately turned to confer with his advisers. After some shoulder-shrugging and

When Paul appealed to Caesar from the tribunal of Festus, it was to the Roman emperor Nero, who ruled from 54 to 68 A.D. This bust of Nero stands today in the Capitoline Museum at Rome. He was emperor during the great fire of Rome in 64 A.D., and was also the first persecutor of the Christians.

head-nodding from them, Festus faced the prisoner with his decision: "You have appealed to Caesar; to Caesar you *shall go*" (25:10). Then he cleared the court.

In the next days Festus had more of a problem than Paul, who suddenly found his long-planned trip to Rome underwritten by the state. Caesar (emperor) at this time was Nero, who, though he already had several crimes to his credit, was not yet the lurid ruler history would come to know so well. In fact, under the guidance of Gallio's brother Seneca, the early years of Nero's reign had been favorable. But one thing Festus dared not do was send Paul on to Rome without a bill of definite charges against him, and such he had been unable to determine.

He raised this problem before the son and daughter of the dead King Agrippa—Herod Agrippa II and his sister Bernice —who had just arrived in Caesarea to pay a visit of welcome to the new governor. Agrippa II was only seventeen when his father died and was deemed too young to succeed him. In the meantime, he had become ruler over lands northeast of Palestine with the near-medical names of Trachonitis and Batanaea, as well as parts of Galilee. His attractive sister Bernice was one of the extraordinary Herodian princesses. Married three times, she was undoubtedly carrying on an incestuous relationship with her brother Agrippa II, and she would eventually become the mistress of no less than Titus, the future Roman emperor.

Interested in hearing Paul speak, this unlikely couple entered the audience hall at their father's one-time palace with great pomp and ceremony for the scheduled interview. When the prisoner was brought in, Festus announced the legal history of Paul's case, including his appeal. Then he added, almost poignantly, "But I have nothing definite to write to my lord [Nero] about him. Therefore I have brought him . . . before you, King Agrippa, that after we have examined him, I may have something to write" (25:26).

Paul offered an impassioned defense, reporting again his

conversion experience and subsequent ministry, culminating in the words:

To this day I have had the help that comes from God, and so I stand here testifying both to small and great, saying nothing but what the prophets and Moses said would come to pass: that the Christ must suffer, and that, by being the first to rise from the dead, he would proclaim light both to the [Jewish] people and to the Gentiles (26:22).

"Paul, you are *mad!*" Festus interrupted. "Your great learning is turning you mad!"

Paul may even have laughed as he brushed off the suggestion. Continuing his focus on Agrippa, he pointed out that the king could corroborate some of his claims, for matters involving Jesus were "not done in a corner." Finally, Paul put it to him point blank: "King Agrippa, do you believe the prophets? I know that you believe . . ."

Agrippa smiled and said, "You think it will not take much to win me over and make a Christian of me!"

"Much or little," said Paul, "I wish to God that not only you, but all those also who are listening to me today, might become what I am, apart from these chains!" (26:28 NEB).

Agrippa II stood up and ended the hearing. When he had retired with Festus and Bernice, he said, "This man is doing nothing to deserve death or imprisonment. If he had not appealed to Caesar, he could have been set free" (26:31).

12

Rome and Nero

And when it was decided that we should sail for Italy, they delivered Paul and some other prisoners to a centurion of the Augustan
Cohort, named Julius.

ACTS 27:1

A ship bound for the Aegean had put in at the port of Caesarea,
and since it was not a military vessel, Aristarchus of Thessalonica and faithful Luke were allowed to sail along with Paul.
Apparently the centurion and his detail of guards had come to
know Paul during his months in prison, for when the ship sailed
off on an overnight run northward to Sidon, Julius allowed him
to go ashore and visit the Christians in that Phoenician port.

From Sidon they had planned a direct northwesterly voyage
toward the Aegean, but stiff winds from that heading made
them sail around the north of Cyprus instead and only then to
the port of Myra in southwestern Asia Minor. There Julius
found a huge Alexandrian grain ship bound for Italy and transferred his party aboard it.

The largest ships afloat on the Mediterranean, such mer-
chantmen worked the famed Egypt-to-Italy grain shuttle,
which sailed during the summer months in a counterclockwise
direction. Leaving the Bay of Naples and heading south with
pottery, metal ware, and passengers, these ships caught the
northwesterly winds beyond Sicily and ran before them directly
to Alexandria in a quick voyage of two weeks or less. Unloading
cargo in Egypt, they took on tons of wheat there and new

passengers, returning to Italy against the winds via a circuitous route that saw them tack past Palestine, Asia Minor, and Greece.

It was on this leg of the shuttle that Paul and 275 other passengers set sail from Myra. A powerful but contrary wind was no help at all. They fairly crept along the south coast of Asia Minor and past Rhodes into the rougher waters of the Aegean. Now no longer shielded by land, they decided to sail under the lee of Crete for shelter from the northwesterlies. Rounding the eastern cape of that island, they coasted along with difficulty until dropping anchor at a small bay called Fair Havens in the south central coast of Crete.

Far enough for that sailing season, Paul concluded, in that so much time had been lost to contrary winds. "Sirs," he told the captain and staff, "I perceive that a [further] voyage will be with injury and much loss, not only of the cargo and the ship, but also of our lives" (27:10). Paul knew the Mediterranean and its habits from boyhood on the sea near Tarsus, as well as from experience: "Three times I have been shipwrecked," he wrote (2 Cor. 11:25). His advice was accurate. Since "the fast had already gone by" (27:9)—i.e., the Day of Atonement in early October—they were now in the danger interim on the Mediterranean beyond what the Romans called *secura navigatio* and near the period of winter's *mare clausum* or "closed sea," from November 10 through March 10.

The owner of the ship happened to be a passenger also, and he discussed Paul's opinion with the captain and Julius, the centurion. They chose to gamble on a last coasting run to a better wintering port on Crete named Phoenix, forty miles farther west, since Fair Havens was little more than a roadstead. A gentle, reliable south wind started blowing, so they weighed anchor and sailed westward with it, close inshore and very carefully. One can almost see Julius jovially tweaking Paul's gray beard on foredeck, suggesting that he stick to preaching after this and leave the navigation to them.

A MEDITERRANEAN STORM

Upon rounding Cape Matala, a vicious Euroclydon suddenly struck them, a violent wind from the east-northeast that area mariners would later call a Levanter. After futile attempts to face into the wind, the crew gave way to it and were driven southwestward across dangerously frothing swells. Just possibly, the two Greek Christians aboard—Luke and Aristarchus— looked backward at 7,000-foot Mt. Ida that seemed to be rolling the gale down on them, wondering wryly if this were the last blast from the pagan gods, since Zeus supposedly grew up on Mt. Ida! Any levity, though, was abruptly swallowed in the ensuing emergency.

Drifting twenty-four miles to the south, they ran under the lee of Cauda, a small island that cut their wind enough to let them hoist up and secure the huge waterlogged lifeboat they had been towing. They also used the relatively calmer waters to reinforce the ship, dropping hawsers crosswise under the hull in U-shaped fashion and then tightening both ends of the cables at center deck.

Once they left the protection of Cauda, the northeaster could have driven them down onto the Syrtes, dangerous shoals off the North African coast, so they lowered their gear, lashing down on deck the sails and rigging except for some small storm sail to keep rudder control for a westerly course as the ship was driven before the wind. The next day, however, they lost all shelter from Crete and found themselves in the center of a seething Mediterranean, the northeaster howling with relentless fury. The pitching and rolling tore pieces of the cargo loose, and they were banging from one side of the hull to the other. Quickly, the crew pitched the loose freight overboard. The next day, since the battered merchantman was taking on some water, they threw overboard even the ship's furniture and whatever tackle could be spared to lighten the vessel.

For more than ten days the storm screamed on, and without

sun by day or stars by night, they had no bearings to fix their location. Eventually, the nauseated, terrified passengers lost all hope of surviving, and—even more horrifying—so did the captain and crew.

At that worst moment Paul gathered them together and said (with a predictable opener):

You should have taken my advice, gentlemen, not to sail from Crete; then you would have avoided this damage and loss. But now I urge you not to lose heart; not a single life will be lost, only the ship. For last night there stood by me an angel of the God whose I am and whom I worship. "Do not be afraid, Paul," he said; "it is ordained that you shall appear before the Emperor; and, be assured, God has granted you the lives of all who are sailing with you." So keep up your courage; I trust in God that it will turn out as I have been told; though we have to be cast ashore on some island (27:21 NEB).

On the fourteenth night of the storm, the sailors suspected that land was near, probably from the roar of nearby surf. They sounded and found twenty fathoms; then, several moments later, fifteen. Rushing to the stern, they threw out four anchors to hold the ship off any rocks ahead. When the anchors finally caught on the seabottom, it marked the first time since Crete that they had the ship under full control.

Squinting in the darkness, they saw either surf or points of lamplight in the distance. It *was* land! Word raced along the deck, and soon the crew were lowering the great lifeboat to escape ship. Paul caught them at it.

"We're laying out anchors from the bow," one of the seamen explained, though Paul knew it was a lie. Calling Julius, he said, "Unless these men stay in the ship, you cannot be saved." Now with implicit faith in Paul's judgment, the centurion had his men cut away the ropes of the lifeboat.

Near dawn Paul addressed passengers and crew, urging them to eat something, as he himself promptly did, giving thanks to God. They followed his example, heartened at the proximate landfall. Then they lightened the ship still more, throwing the

St. Paul's Shoal and St. Paul's Bay on the north shore of the island of Malta. A statue of the apostle stands atop the island at left center today, commemorating the famous shipwreck.

remaining wheat cargo into the sea.

When day broke, they saw a bay with a beach dead ahead. Hoisting their foresail and cutting away the anchors, they scudded before the wind until their bow rammed into a shoal at the head of the bay and stuck fast. When the pounding surf started breaking up the stern, the Roman guards drew out their swords to kill the prisoners lest any swim off and escape. Julius, however, vetoed this customary procedure, and instead told all who could swim to plunge into the water and make for shore, while others should float in on planks and debris from the ship. Venturing overboard as ordered, they were pulled out of the swirling surf and onto the beach by friendly natives. Only then did they learn that they had landed on Malta, the smallish island below Sicily.

MALTA

That all 276 people on shipboard should have been saved in such a fashion may seem incredible, but a visit to that landfall today on the northern shore of Malta suggests that "St. Paul's Shoal" within "St. Paul's Bay" are sites not only correctly named, but so near surrounding shores that loss of life from drowning could indeed have been prevented, especially with friendly Maltese wading out to assist them.

Other islanders were busy building a bonfire on the beach to warm the survivors, since a cold drizzle had started. Paul helped out by gathering a bundle of sticks and throwing them on the fire when suddenly he felt a painful stinging in his hand. Fastened to it was an ugly viper, driven out of the fagots by the heat! Immediately, he shook the snake off his hand and into the flames.

Anyone else might have done the same, but would soon have suffered painful swelling, loss of consciousness, and then death, like Cleopatra of Egypt, who was bitten by the same species of asp viper. The Maltese assumed that Paul must have been a murderous criminal, marked by the gods for death despite his escape from shipwreck. But when Paul carried on with impunity, the credulous islanders changed their minds and deemed him a god!

Several miles south of the bonfire lay the estate of Publius, chief magistrate of Malta, who hosted Paul and his companions for their first three days on the island. Publius' father lay ill with dysentery and fever, but when Paul laid his hands on him, he was cured. Word of the healing spread quickly across Malta, and Paul had a busy ministry during the three months they wintered on the island.

In late February or early March of 58 or 59 A.D.—Pauline chronology is still not absolute—the survivors set sail in the *Dioscuri*, another great Alexandrian grain ship that had wintered in Malta. It was named for the Twin Brothers, the gods Castor and Pollux, who were adorning its prow as wooden figureheads. This time their brief voyage was simple and traceable, as they put in at Syracuse on Sicily and then Rhegium at the toe of the Italian boot. There they waited for a reliable south wind to carry them through the Straits of Messina without foundering on the rock and whirlpool there, Homer's fabled Scylla and Charybdis. When a spring breeze developed, they easily ran with it through the straits and up to the Bay of Naples.

Gliding past Capri toward evening, they may well have seen the breast-shaped hulk of Mt. Vesuvius lording it over the eastern shore of the bay. In just a score of years it would rumble into life and bury the towns of Herculaneum and Pompeii nestled near its base in a cataclysm of mud, lava, and fiery ash. Now the *Dioscuri* reached its destination, the commercial port of Puteoli in the north shore of the Bay of Naples. Today it is called Pozzuoli, and ruins of the market hall there show one of the first buildings Paul would have seen after landing, since it faces the waterfront.

If the year of Paul's arrival were 59, and if his ship set sail from Malta on March 10—maritime insurance could have been vitiated by any earlier voyage during *mare clausum*—then one of the most bizarre coincidences in ancient history could well have occurred, which has thus far escaped scholarly notice. The run from Malta to Puteoli, with stops at the various ports of call cited in Acts 28:12 ff., probably took about nine or ten days, making the estimated date for Paul's arrival at the Bay of Naples the evening of March 20. Something else was happening several miles west of Paul's ship that very night. The emperor Nero had just given his mother a banquet at Baiae, his villa on the western rim of the bay, and then seen her off at his dock for a short cruise across the bay to the villa where she was staying. Unfortunately, her boat was nothing less than a collapsible cabin cruiser, rigged so that its ceiling would cave in and crush her to death. If that failed, levers would open the hull and sink the ship.

As it happened, neither device worked properly, and Nero's mother saved herself by diving off the ship and swimming in the bay until rescued by some oyster fishermen, who brought her safely back to her villa on shore. By dawn, however, a detail of Nero's marines stormed into the villa and clubbed her to death anyway, as she lay in her bed.

Paul obviously could not know of the mortal events taking

The port of Puteoli, where Paul and his party landed at the Bay of Naples. The city is called Pozzuoli today.

One of the first structures Paul would have seen upon disembarking at Puteoli was the *macellum* or covered market, the ruins of which survive from the first century A.D. At center is the circular base of a temple to Serapis.

place just west of his ship while it was docking in Puteoli, and of course this coincidence is neither proved nor provable. But it does point out, ominously enough, the sort of Caesar Paul had appealed to!

Christians were already established at Puteoli—Paul's fame had preceded him there—and the missionaries were invited to stay with them for a time. In an extraordinary concession Julius allowed Paul a week in Puteoli, unquestionably a favor in return for Paul's crucial services on the voyage. It may be from this early congregation that the faith expanded around the Bay of Naples, because there were Christians in nearby Herculaneum shortly afterward. One of the houses in that resort town, today liberated from its lava burial by Mt. Vesuvius, shows the clear outlines of a metal cross that had been set in the wall over a charred *prie-dieu* in an upstairs room. The cross evidently is just as old a Christian symbol as the fish.

The final leg of Paul's journey was beautiful in the early Italian spring. Soon their highway merged with the Appian Way, the famous artery that led them northward to Rome. At the forty-third milestone was a place called Forum of Appius. Both here and ten miles farther on at a village named Three Taverns, Paul, Luke, and Aristarchus were happily surprised to find a delegation from the Christians of Rome. The church there had been alerted to his arrival, and possibly many of the names found in Romans 16 were clustering along the sides of the Appian Way in a grand welcoming committee. What enormously cheered the travelers must have astonished Julius.

IMPERIAL ROME

At last they reached the great capital of the Mediterranean world, Paul's planned destination for years. Julius conducted his group northward past the Circus Maximus and the Forum, stopping finally at the Castra Praetoria on the northeastern fringe of Rome. Here he reported to the commandant of the camp of the Praetorian Guard, delivering his prisoners and the

A primitive Christian oratory in the upper room of the so-called
"House of the Bicentenary" at Herculaneum. A whitish stuccoed
panel shows the imprint of a large cross, probably metallic, that had
been removed or possibly used as a stamping device. Before it are the
remains of a small wooden altar, charred by lava from the eruption
of Mt. Vesuvius in 79 A.D.

documents of indictment on them. He may well have had a few generous things to say about Paul to the commandant, for Luke adds that after registering, "Paul was allowed to stay by himself with the soldier that guarded him . . . in his own hired dwelling," doubtless nearby in northeastern Rome (28:16, 30).

Only three days elapsed between the close of Paul's momentous journey and his resumption of mission work. Barely settled, he invited the local Jewish leaders to his rented abode and candidly introduced himself, his faith, and his mission.

"We have received no letters from Judea about you," the Jewish leaders replied, "and none of the brethren coming here has reported or spoken any evil about you. But . . . with regard to this sect we know that everywhere it is spoken against" (28:21). Open-mindedly, however, the leaders of the Roman synagogues agreed with Paul on a day when they would bring their members in to hear him.

At the appointed time they came to his lodging in large numbers. In perhaps his ultimate effort to Christianize Jewry, Paul lectured all day on Jesus as fulfillment of the Law and the Prophets, but with the same familiar results. With some exceptions, the Jews were not convinced, and Paul told them wistfully: "Let it be known to you then that this salvation of God has been sent to the Gentiles; they will listen."

Luke closes this scene—and alas the Book of Acts—with the following intriguing verse:

And he [Paul] lived there two whole years at his own expense, and welcomed all who came to him, preaching the kingdom of God and teaching about the Lord Jesus Christ quite openly and unhindered (28:30).

What happened then, Luke? What was Paul's fate? Peter's? Yours? What about the great fire of Rome just three years after you break off your account? And Nero's horrible persecution of the Christians? And—

No serious reader of the New Testament has failed to fire these queries at the "beloved physician," and his less-than-

The Appian Way near Rome, with ruins of patrician tombs alongside the highway and the moon overhead.

satisfactory conclusion has been explained in various ways. Some have conjectured that Luke wrote an as-yet-undiscovered *2 Acts,* and many Biblical scholars dream of finding an ancient scroll that would begin: "This *third* treatise, O Theophilus. . . ." (That gentleman, of course, was the man to whom Luke addressed both his Gospel and the Acts. He may have been an unknown Roman official, or possibly any "friend of God," as his Greek name translates.)

Second Acts, however, is unlikely. Aside from the dozen other explanations for what may have happened, another reading of the concluding verse shows that it is not only quite ahead of its time literarily ("Leave 'em wondering"), but is, in fact, honest and satisfactory after all: Luke's great purpose was merely to show how the gospel spread from Jerusalem to Rome. And he did that.

PAUL'S LAST YEARS

Other sources shed some light on Paul's fate—his own writings, for example. During his detention in Rome, he most likely wrote his famed "prison epistles": *Philippians, Colossians, Ephesians,* and *Philemon.* Passages in these attest to the astonishing success of his mission in the imperial capital, despite his confinement. To the church at Philippi he wrote: "I want you to know, brethren, that what has happened to me has really served to advance the gospel, so that it has become known throughout the whole Praetorian Guard and to all the rest that my imprisonment is for Christ" (1:12). There was even a Christian group growing in the palace itself, for Paul closes: "All the saints greet you, especially those of Caesar's household" (4:22). Such claims to the growth of the faith could hardly be inflated, because in only four years that "vast multitude" of Christians would be persecuted, according to the pagan author Tacitus. In this same, revealing letter Paul seems confident of visiting Philippi in the near future (2:24), and he may indeed have done so.

Surveying all the evidence and clues available from the sources, the following seems to have been Paul's legal fate. The long delay of his hearing before Nero—two years—was due probably less to any crowded court docket and more to the imperial court's decision to wait until Paul's accusers arrived from Judea, because the documents indicting him—if they actually survived the shipwreck at Malta!—would have been in a *very* messy condition both as to form and content. Festus had been worried about the problem of sending along with Paul a *clear* statement of charges against him, and the hearing before Agrippa and Bernice hardly achieved that. In fairness to the prosecution, then, witnesses from Judea may have been invited to come testify against Paul in Rome. That they did not bother to do so, at least for two years, is quite understandable. Paul's was no longer a *cause célèbre.* His chief prosecutor, the high priest Ananias, had been deposed, and his successor may not have been interested in the case. Those who were, among the Sanhedrists, must have realized that their charges were flimsy, particularly on the alleged defilement of the Temple. While flimsy charges could be pressed at home, it would have been dangerous to press them in the capital of the Empire, where such legal conduct was penalized.

Paul's opponents in Palestine, then, could achieve much more by doing nothing at all, for this would leave their man, not "turning in the breeze" but in a peculiar limbo legally. Incredibly, Roman law did not really cover a situation in which a person's accusers failed to appear to support their indictment, since Roman *accusatores,* or their representatives, regularly seem to have made their appearance.

Nevertheless, Paul undoubtedly did finally face Nero himself for trial, because Acts 27:24 clearly presupposes this. What probably happened, accordingly, is that one of Paul's more powerful Roman friends pressed the case for him, and he eventually had his day in court. Working from the documents of indictment (again, *if* they survived), some Jewish or Roman prosecutor would have raised the three original charges first lodged against Paul at Caesarea by Tertullus. Allowing another party to renew an accusation in the absence of the original accusers was permitted under Roman law at this time (*Digestae,* xlviii, 16, x, 2).

For his part Paul would have offered a by-now predictable defense, including the episode on the Damascus Road, which might have made the superstitious Nero a bit uncomfortable. And although he had eliminated his mother and his list of crimes was growing, Nero had not yet reached the stage of dissipation and cruelty associated with his later reign. Accordingly, with Paul's eloquence on the one hand, and the less than impressive charges on the other, Nero may indeed have acquitted the apostle—particularly if, as seems likely, the philosopher Seneca and respected senators were serving as imperial assessors in helping decide the case. At this point, too, the Roman

Model of Nero's Vatican hippodrome, site of the first Christian persecution. The obelisk on the *spina* stands today at the center of the colonnade in front of St. Peter's basilica at the Vatican (see final photograph).

state had not yet declared Christianity illegal.

Although some important scholars disagree, there is strong, though not conclusive, evidence that Paul was actually acquitted after his first trial at Rome and subsequently visited both Spain in the West and his beloved mission churches in the East. The pastoral epistles, *1* and *2 Timothy* and *Titus,* cannot be fitted satisfactorily into the three missionary journeys, and they tell of Paul's later activities in the Aegean world, although the authenticity of the pastorals is much debated. Clement of Rome, however, in his Epistle to the Corinthians of 96 A.D., asserts that Paul "reached the limits of the West" before he died, which, for a Roman author, would imply Spain or Portugal. Romans 15 shows that Paul had surely planned a trip to Spain via Rome, and a second-century document, the *Canon*

The road on which Paul most probably traveled to his martyrdom led from the Ostian Gate (today called the Gate of San Paolo) at the southwestern corner of Rome, past the pyramid tomb of Gaius Cestius (d. 12 B.C.), and out on the Ostian Way at the lower part of the photograph. This model, as the previous, is part of the vast scaled reconstruction of ancient Rome at the Museo della Civiltà Romana in Rome.

Muratorii, speaks of "Paul's journey when he set out from Rome for Spain" (xxxviii).

If he did visit Spain, Paul would next have returned eastward to confirm the believers in a "fourth missionary journey" to the Aegean. Titus refers to his work on the island of Crete, and the other pastorals have him back in Greece and Asia Minor. There, for some reason, he was arrested a second time and sent to face Nero once again. A postscript found in some later manuscripts of 2 Timothy states that it was "written from Rome, when Paul was brought before Nero the second time."

Now, about 66–67 A.D., Paul would have been in mortal danger when he stood before Nero, whatever the indictments that brought him there. Because two years earlier the emperor, in deflecting from himself the public outcry that he had set Rome ablaze, blamed the Christians for arson, as noted, and tortured them to death. Being a Christian now carried the death penalty, so Nero or his justices could hardly acquit this strange and troublesome *leader* of the Christians.

This time Paul had no illusions about being freed, as 2 Timothy shows so poignantly. When his last day had come, the apostle was presumably accompanied in his final journey across Rome to the Ostian Gate by a grieving group of friends who had survived the cruel first wave of persecution. Several miles beyond the Gate, on the road to the port of Ostia, stood the chopping block. While the sword was being prepared by the executioner (Roman citizens were not crucified), Paul doubtless made a last statement. His words were probably similar to what he had written earlier to his young co–worker, Timothy:

The time of my departure has come. I have fought the good fight, I have finished the race, I have kept the faith. Henceforth there is laid up for me the crown of righteousness, which the Lord, the righteous judge, will award to me on that Day, and not only to me but also to all who have loved his appearing (2 Tim. 4:6).

The blade dropped, the apostle died—the greatest missionary, the greatest theologian in the history of Christianity, and

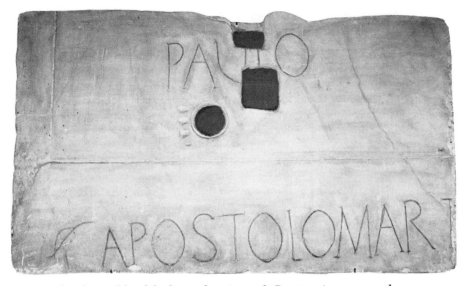

A whitish marble slab from the time of Constantine covers the presumed sepulcher of Paul in the basilica of St. Paul's Outside-the-Walls at Rome. The inscription in red—"To Paul, Apostle and Martyr"—shows fourth-century lettering style. The slab measures 1.27 by 2.12 meters, and is 4.5 meters above the sarcophagus. The round aperture at the center is the most ancient of the perforations, and was used to lower and replace an incense burner at the annual Feast of St. Paul. The rectangular openings above it were made later to permit the faithful to lower objects into the tomb area, which they regarded with veneration afterward.

the one who had universalized its message.

Sustained by the resurrection hope that was the culmination of all his preaching, Paul's friends buried him nearby, along the Ostian Way. The much-traveled apostle would have appreciated that gesture—burial alongside a highway. Today the road connects Rome with her international airport at Ostia.

The early church fathers—Clement, Tertullian, Origen, and others—all agree that Paul was finally executed by the Roman government, and no tradition disputes that he met his end along the Ostian Way just outside of Rome. The magnificent basilica of St. Paul's Outside the Walls now stands over the presumed place where he was buried. It is erected over earlier memorial structures dating back to the time of Constantine. Under the high altar of the basilica is a slab on which the lettering "PAVLO APOSTOLO MART" indicates an early Christian memorial "To Paul, Apostle and Martyr."

PETER'S LAST YEARS

This, of course, is only Paul's story, and parts of it were being replicated elsewhere in the Mediterranean by the other apostles. In most earliest church histories the focus is inevitably on Paul because of his centrality in the Acts account, and one wishes that similar sources were extant on the early Christian efforts elsewhere.

Only sketchy information survives on the later years of Simon Peter, "prince of the apostles." His last mention in Acts shows him defending Paul at the Jerusalem Council (15:7), but reflections of his activity appear in Antioch, Corinth, and eventually Rome. The provenance of the persecution documents *1* and *2 Peter* is Rome, not literally "Babylon" (I, 5:13), which is the cryptic name for Rome in apocalyptic literature. Indeed, earliest church tradition as well as archaeology point to Peter's presence in Rome at the close of his ministry and his martyrdom there, probably before Paul's. Clement's letter to Corinth strongly links the martyrdoms of Peter and Paul with those of the Roman Christians enduring the Neronian persecution, and a short time later, in 107 A.D., Ignatius of Antioch's letter to Rome contains the telling phrase: "Not like Peter and Paul do I give you [Roman Christians] commands" (iv, 3).

In the next century there are numerous references to the martyrdoms of Peter and Paul in Rome, and one of these is particularly interesting. The church historian Eusebius cites a second-century presbyter, Gaius of Rome, who stated: "I can point out the monuments [or trophies] of the apostles: for if you will go to the Vatican hill or to the Ostian Way, you will find the monuments of those [Peter and Paul] who founded the church." The monuments marked the traditional sites of their martyrdoms and likely their places of burial as well, since Gaius was countering a claim from Asia of apostolic *tombs* in that province. Constantine later erected the basilicas of St. Peter and St. Paul respectively at these locations, where the newer so-named structures that replaced them stand today.

That Peter was martyred in Rome is supported by a great majority of modern scholars, even though they still argue over the time, place, and nature of that martyrdom. From various indications it seems to have been in connection with Nero's persecution, and there is no dispute over where that series of tortures was inflicted. Because the vast Circus Maximus had been scorched in the great fire of Rome (and the Colosseum had not yet been built), Nero staged his spectacle across the Tiber in the Vatican Valley, where he had gardens and a private hippodrome for racing his horses. It was here that the grisly scene was played out, as recorded—not by a Christian hagiographer—but by a pagan author, Cornelius Tacitus:

A farce was made of their deaths. Dressed in the skins of wild animals, they [the Christians] were torn to death by dogs; or they were fastened to crosses, and when daylight ended, were burned to serve as torches by night. Nero had provided his gardens for the spectacle (*Annals* xv, 44).

The emperor Caligula had imported a lofty obelisk from Egypt and set it up in the central *spina* of his hippodrome across the Tiber, which Nero had inherited and enlarged. If this obelisk had eyes, it would have witnessed the lurid persecution of the Christians above, and probably the crucifixion of Peter also. If it had a tongue, the obelisk could tell us about it, because today it stands at the center of the great circular colonnade in front of St. Peter's basilica at Rome.

THE OTHER APOSTLES

Mark, happily, was reconciled again with Paul in Rome (Col. 4:10) where, according to the church fathers, he also served as Peter's secretary and composed the earliest Gospel bearing his name under Peter's influence. Tradition also has Mark the founder of the Christian church in Alexandria, Egypt.

James, brother of Jesus and first bishop of the Jerusalem church, is credited with authoring the New Testament letter bearing his name, but in 62 A.D. he met the same fate as Stephen. Josephus tells the story. Festus, Paul's last judge at Caesarea, died in office, and before Nero could send his successor to Palestine, the high priest in Jerusalem, Ananus, took it upon himself to indict James before the Sanhedrin, which condemned the apostle and several others to death by stoning. It should be noted that these executions took place in the *absence* of the new Roman governor, who was later so angry at such arrogation of power by Ananus that he was dismissed from office. This item, from a non-Christian source, should be recalled by some misguided scholars today who would seek to deprive the Sanhedrin of all responsibility for opposing Jesus and the early Christians and transfer it to the Romans instead.

John, "the beloved disciple," carried his ministry to Ephesus, according to early church tradition, where he also acted as dutiful foster son to Mary, the mother of Jesus, a role assigned to him at Calvary. To avoid persecution by the emperor Domitian, John for a time took refuge on the tiny Aegean isle of Patmos, where tradition has him composing the Book of *Revelation,* after which he returned to Ephesus. Here, presumably, he authored the Fourth Gospel and the letters bearing his name.

The other apostles fanned out elsewhere, according to various traditions. Barnabas missionized the islands; Peter's brother Andrew went to the north shore of the Black Sea, Scythia then, Russia today; Thaddaeus preached in Syria and

The 84-foot obelisk that witnessed Nero's first great persecution of the Christians. The emperor Caligula had brought it to Rome from Heliopolis in Egypt, and set it up in the hippodrome at the Ager Vaticanus, where it graced the *spina* of that racecourse under Nero. Later, the obelisk was crowned with a cross and transferred in 1586 to its present location at the center of the semicircular colonnade in front of St. Peter's basilica at the Vatican.

Armenia; Bartholomew and Thomas in Persia and India. Upon finishing his church history and the Gospel named for him, Luke possibly labored in Bithynia. Matthew, his coevangelist, also completed his Gospel and then carried the Good News to both Jews and Gentiles before enduring probable persecution and death. Silas, Paul's companion on the second journey, filled a similar role with Peter and then served as missionary to northern Asia Minor. Church traditions also have Timothy ministering to western Asia Minor from Ephesus, while Titus preached in Crete and Dalmatia, today's Yugoslavia.

All of the apostles endured great hardships for the faith, many suffering martyrdom itself. Not one of them could see the ultimate triumph of Christianity—except through the eyes of faith and the inspiration of the same Spirit who arrived with the first Pentecost and never withdrew. Though at the time the Christian cause seemed persecuted, burned, crucified, beheaded, and even eaten out of existence by the greatest power in the world, a greater power was at work that would see Christianity conquer Rome a little more than two centuries later, and "the ends of the earth" after that, in Jesus' own prediction.

It was Christ, not Caesar, who captured the future.

✑Notes

1. The Commission

AUGUSTUS: Suetonius, *Augustus* xcix. The emperor's *very* last statement, just after the quotation in the text, was: "Forty young men are carrying me off," an indication that his wits were wandering, though just possibly a reference to the Praetorian honor guard at his funeral.

LUKE: Paul calls him "the beloved physician" in Col. 4:14. That he was a Gentile seems strongly indicated in Col. 4:10 ff., where Luke is grouped outside those "of the circumcision."

2. The Day of Pentecost

PENTECOST: This festival, among the Jews, did not commemorate the giving of the Law, as some would have it, until after 200 A.D., when it became also a feast of revelation.—The date suggested for the first Christian Pentecost, May 25, A.D. 33, is based on the presumption of April 5 of that year for the first Easter. The chronology of Holy Week is further discussed in Jack Finegan, *Handbook of Biblical Chronology* (Princeton, 1964), pp. 259 ff., and Paul L. Maier, "Sejanus, Pilate, and the Date of the Crucifixion," *Church History*, XXXVII (March, 1968), 1–11; and *First Easter* (Harper & Row, 1973), p. 124.

JOSEPHUS: His statistic on the population of Jerusalem during the high festivals is 3,000,000 for the Passover of 65 A.D. (*Wars* ii, 14, 3). At least he is consistent with himself, because later Josephus reports 256,500 paschal lambs slaughtered at a subsequent Passover. At twelve people per lamb, this would come to 3,078,000 (*Wars* vi, 9, 3). Nearly all scholars reduce such figures to several hundred thousands.

TACITUS: His famous reference to the Christian persecutions under Nero is *Annals* xv, 44. Attempts have been made to discredit this passage as a Christian interpolation, but they have failed, and most scholars regard the passage as authentic.

3. The Opposition

GAMALIEL: Judaic references to him are the tractates *Gittin* 4, 2; *Rosh Hashanah* 2, 5; and *Sotah* 9, 15 which states: "When Rabban Gamaliel the Elder died, the glory of the law ceased and purity and abstinence died." The reference to Theudas' insurrection as taking place before that of Judas in Luke's version of Gamaliel's speech (Acts 5:36 ff.) conflicts with evidence from Josephus, *Antiquities* [hereafter *Antiq.*] xx, 5, 1, who places the revolt of Judas in 6 A.D. and Theudas' after 44 A.D. Possibly there was an earlier Theudas.

4. The Dispersion

GITTA: This is suggested as site for Philip's activities because it is one of the few towns in hilly Samaria to which one would go *down* (Acts 8:5) from the Jerusalem plateau. Justin Martyr also associates Gitta with the activities of Simon Magus in *Apologia* i, 26, 56.

SIMON MAGUS: Eusebius, *Ecclesiastical History* ii, 13, 1–8; Justin Martyr, *loc. cit.;* Irenaeus, *Adversus Haereses* i, 23, 1–2.

5. Peter The Rock

THE ITALIAN COHORT: For the identity and full name of the *Cohors II Italica* see "Cohors" in Georg Wissowa, ed., *Paulys Real-Encyclopädie der classischen Altertumswissenschaft* (Stuttgart: Metzlersche Verlag, 1953 ff.), VII, pp. 304 ff. (This massive reference work also has articles on most of the proper names cited in the text.) There is some debate on whether the Italian Cohort could have been in Judea prior to Vespasian, but also scholarly support for the implication in Acts that it must have been in Caesarea by this time.

HEROD AGRIPPA I: References outside the NT include: Josephus, *Antiq.* xviii and xix. This is also the sole source of information on Agrippa and the interregnum at Rome following the death of Caligula.—Josephus makes no mention of the embassy from Tyre and Sidon reported in Acts. The two citations in the text regarding the strange death of Agrippa are Louis H. Feldman's translation of Josephus, *Antiq.* xix, 8, 2, in the *Loeb Classical Library.* Used by permission.

THE THEATER AT CAESAREA: Some scholars hold that Agrippa made his appearance at one of the as-yet-unexcavated amphitheaters at Caesarea. Josephus, however, identifies the place as *to theatron,* not *amphitheatron* at *loc. cit.* Since 44 A.D. would have been the wrong year for the quinquennial games at Caesarea, this spectacle was probably in honor of Claudius' birthday and on a smaller scale. See F. F. Bruce, *New Testament History* (Doubleday, 1971), p. 263.

6. Saul The Fanatic

TENTMAKING: An alternate interpretation of the Greek *skenopoios* (18:3) is "leatherworker," according to the first Latin translation of this passage as well as several early church fathers. Because Paul's home province was famous for *cilicium,* however, "tentmaker" would seem the preferable, as it is the more literal, translation.

ESCAPE FROM DAMASCUS: Though Acts does not mention the Nabataean involvement against Saul, nor indeed his three-year sojourn in the Arabian desert, Paul himself cites the latter in Gal. 1:17–18 and the former in 2 Cor. 11:32 ff., which demonstrates that his basket escape took place after his *second* visit to Damascus following the visit to Arabia. The Aretas cited is Aretas IV of Petra, whose daughter had married, and been jilted by, Herod Antipas (Josephus, *Antiq.* xviii, 5, 1).

7. Paul's First Journey

SERGIUS PAULUS: "L. Sergius Paullus" is listed as the third of five "*curator[es riparum] et alv[ei Tiberis]*" under Claudius in *CIL* VI, 31545. Another inscription discovered at Soloi in northern Cyprus mentions a "*Paulos [. . . anth]upatos,*" though whether this refers to Sergius Paulus is disputed (*IGR* III, 930).

BAUCIS AND PHILEMON: Ovid, *Metamorphoses* viii, 611 ff.

8. Quarrels And Controversy

THE JERUSALEM COUNCIL: The apostolic conclave of Acts 15 is most probably the same as that recorded by Paul in Galatians 2. Despite differences in reportage, the theological issue in both versions is identical. Titus, as one of the delegates, is cited only in Gal. 2:1.

9. Paul's Second Journey

TIMOTHY: His circumcision (Acts 16:1 ff.) was not inconsistent in that he was considered a Jew because his mother was Jewish.

ACTS 17 TEXT AND COMMENTARY: Some of this material first appeared in Paul L. Maier, "Acts 17," *The Lutheran Witness*, 93 (June 16, 1974), 8–9. Used by permission.

THE AREOPAGUS: An alternate site for Paul's address is the *Stoa Basileios* in the Athenian agora, where the *Court* of Areopagus sometimes met. Whether Acts intends "Areopagus" as Mars' Hill or as court is not clear, although most incline to the former.

L. JUNIUS GALLIO: His "hook" remark is attested by Dio Cassius lx, 35. See also lxii, 25; Pliny, *Natural History* xxxi, 62; Seneca, *Epistulae Morales* civ, 1; Tacitus, *Annals* xv, 73. The Delphi inscription is published in Dittenberger, ed., *Sylloge Inscriptionum Graecorum*, Ed. 3, 801 D.

CORINTH: The excavations there are reported in American School of Classical Studies at Athens, *Ancient Corinth, A Guide to the Excavations* (6th ed., 1954); H. J. Cadbury, "Erastus of Corinth," *Journal of Biblical Literature*, L (1931), 42 ff.; and "The *Macellum* of Corinth," *ibid.*, LIII (1934), 34 ff.

10. Paul's Third Journey

THOMAS: Eusebius, *Ecclesiastical History* iii, 1.

GALATIANS: Paul's letter to them is difficult to date. Some scholars place it just after his return from the First Missionary Journey, making it, not 1 Thessalonians, the earliest of his epistles. But in view of the report in Gal. 2 on what is undoubtedly the Jerusalem Council, a majority of scholars date the letter at the close of the Second or during the Third Missionary Journey, since its content is so similar to Romans and the Corinthian epistles.—As to the other problem involving Galatia as a geographical term, the so-called North Galatian hypothesis—which claims that Paul visited northern Asia Minor and the Celtic tribes there—seems very unlikely, because the apostle would have had to communicate with them in Celtic, not Greek.

GLOSSOLALIA: Parts of this discussion first appeared in Paul L. Maier, "Tongues Have Been Here Before," *Christian Herald*, 98 (October, 1975), 16–22. Used by permission.

11. Jeopardy in Jerusalem

TEMPLE STELE: Josephus, *Antiq.* xv, 11, 5. Titus' statement about the warnings is cited in Josephus, *Wars* vi, 2, 4.

EGYPTIAN PSEUDO-PROPHET: Josephus, *Wars* ii, 13, 5.

ANANIAS BEN-NEBEDEUS: Josephus, *Antiq.* xx, 5, 2; *Wars* ii, 17, 9. The Babylonian Talmud also charges him with gluttony in *Pesahim* 57a. Cp. *Kerithoth* 28b.

FELIX: Tacitus, *Annals* xii, 54; *Histories* v, 9; Josephus, *Antiq.* xx, 7, 1 ff.; Suetonius, *Claudius* xxviii. The son of Felix is not named, but his death in the eruption of Vesuvius is reported in *Antiq.* xx, 7, 2.

AGRIPPA II AND BERNICE: Josephus, *Antiq.* xix, 9, 2; xx, 5, 2; 7, 3; *Wars* ii, 16, 4 *et passim;* Suetonius, *Titus* vii; Dio Cassius lxvi, 15.

12. Rome and Nero

NERO'S PLOT: The emperor had used the Festival of Minerva, celebrated March 19 to 23, as a pretext for inviting his mother, Agrippina the Younger, down to Baiae for a banquet of reconciliation, since they had become estranged, suspecting each other of plots. The collapsible cabin cruiser ride seems to have taken place on the second night of the festival, or March 20. Cp. Suetonius, *Nero* xxviii; Tacitus, *Annals* xiv, 3–5; Dio Cassius lxi, 12–13.

THE PRAETORIAN COMMANDANT: The Western version of the Greek text at Acts 28:16 has an interesting variation: "When we came to Rome, the centurion handed the prisoners over to the commandant of the camp [*to stratopedarcho*], and Paul was ordered to remain by himself with the soldiers who were guarding him." In commenting on this variant, Theodor Mommsen equated the Greek term with the Latin *princeps peregrinorum*, the chief of a special logistics supply corps who lived in a camp on the Caelian. See Th. Mommsen and Ad. Harnack, "Zu Apostelgesch. 28,16," *Sitzungsberichte der Kön. Preussischen Akademie der Wissenschaften zu Berlin* (1895), 491 ff. But A. N. Sherwin-White more aptly suggests *princeps castrorum*, "commandant of the camp" (of the Praetorians), as the best translation for *stratopedarchos*. See Sherwin-White, *Roman Society and Roman Law in the New Testament* (Oxford: Clarendon, 1963), pp. 108 ff.

THE PRISON EPISTLES: Whether they were written from Ephesus, Caesarea, or Rome is still debated, but a growing scholarly consensus leans strongly to the last, particularly because an Ephesian imprisonment is questionable, and Phil. 1:12 ff. and 4:22 point almost conclusively to Rome.

CLEMENT: 1 Clement v, 1–7; cp. Strabo, *Geographica* ii, 1. Clement's linking the martyrdoms of Peter and Paul with the Roman Christians is 1 Clement v and vi.

EUSEBIUS AND GAIUS: *Ecclesiastical History* ii, 25.

PETER'S CRUCIFIXION: The apocryphal *Acts of Peter,* dated about 200 A.D., contain the moving legend that Peter was leaving Rome to escape Nero's persecution when he met Jesus along the Appian Way. *"Domine, quo vadis?"* asked Peter, "Lord, where are you going?" Jesus replied, "I go to Rome, to be crucified again." At which Peter, shamed one last time by Jesus, turned back toward Rome to endure martyrdom. However, one thing about the legend certainly is *not* true: Peter and Jesus would never have been speaking Latin to each other but Aramaic.

Similarly, the legend that Peter was crucified by Nero head-downward because he did not deem himself worthy to suffer exactly as Jesus did is possible, but seems an embellishment. It was Origen, as quoted by Eusebius, *op. cit.,* iii, 1, who first commented on the head-downward position of the apostle. No early Roman tradition reports Peter as crucified this way, even if such a position was not unknown. See Seneca, *ad Marciam* xx.

DEATH OF JAMES: Josephus, *Antiq.* xx, 9, 1.

OTHER APOSTOLIC MINISTRIES: Eusebius, *Ecclesiastical History* iii, 1.

HIEBERT LIBRARY

3 6877 00039 2661

14539

BR
165
M26
1976

Maier, Paul L.

First Christians

DATE			
OCT 15 '89			
MY 8 '91			
AP 27 '92			
JE 9 '92			
AP 15 '93			
MY 27 '94			
MY 2 '94			

HIEBERT LIBRARY
Pacific College - M. B. Seminary
Fresno, Calif. 93702

© THE BAKER & TAYLOR CO.